John Heath-Stub

John Heath-Stubbs was born in 1918 and educated at Queens College, Oxford. A critic, anthologist and translator as well as a poet, he has received the Queen's Gold Medal for Poetry and the prestigious Cross of St Augustine. Carcanet published seven previous collections by Heath-Stubbs, as well as a *Collected Poems* and a collection of his literary essays. In 1988 he was awarded the OBE. His poetry was published by Carcanet for almost thirty years. He died in London in December 2006.

John Clegg was born in Chester in 1986, and grew up in Cambridge where he now lives. In 2013, he won an Eric Gregory Award. His PhD is from the University of Durham. His collection *Holy Toledo!* was published by Carcanet in 2016. John Clegg works as a bookseller and a literary sleuth in London.

Carcanet Classics include

Beowulf translated by Chris McCully
Dictator/Gilgamesh adapted by Philip Terry
Gilgamesh Retold by Jenny Lewis
Pearl translated by Jane Draycott
Edmund Blunden *Selected Poems* edited by Robyn Marsack
Catullus *The Books of Catullus* edited and translated
by Simon Smith
Rebecca Elson *A Responsibility to Awe: Collected Poems*
Walter Pater *Selected Essays* edited by Alex Wong
Propertius *Poems* translated by James Womack
Arthur Rimbaud *Illuminations* translated by John Ashbery
George Seferis *Collected Poems*
Charles Tomlinson *Swimming Chenango Lake: Selected Poems*
edited by David Morley
William Carlos Williams *Collected Poems volumes I and II*

Selected Poems

JOHN HEATH-STUBBS

edited by John Clegg

Carcanet
Classics

First published in Great Britain in 2018 in the Carcanet Classics series by
Carcanet Press Ltd
Alliance House, 30 Cross Street
Manchester M2 7AQ
www.carcanet.co.uk

A CIP catalogue record for this book is
available from the British Library,
ISBN 978 1 784106 47 8

The publisher acknowledges financial assistance from Arts Council England.

Typeset in England by XL Publishing Services, Exmouth
Printed and bound in England by SRP Ltd, Exeter

Dedicatory Poem

to Guthrie McKie

These poems are objects not subjects, made
From a twist of words, a moment of the mind's freedom.
Like midges, they hum and dance
In the warm air, whose larvae
Were bred for long in the damp soil.
That soil is my black moods, my weeks of silence:
You have had to deal with those, it is only just
You get the poems as well.
Here I deliver them, along with –
Oh, I almost forgot to add – my love.

(from *Naming the Beasts*, 1982)

Contents

Preface

This is a short selection from a very large body of work. The pre-1965 poetry, which I have selected from freely, was later half-repudiated by the author, I think for bad reasons. Heath-Stubbs's early poems include some of his strongest and most characteristic: 'An Heroic Epistle', 'Mozart' (praised by Hugh Kenner), 'The Divided Ways' and 'Epitaph' belong in any anthology of twentieth-century poetry. The change in style after 'Epitaph' is barely noticeable, and amounts not so much to a rejection of romanticism as a rejection of the dramatic monologue – a shame, as in that mode and a characteristic 'narrated' psychological monologue (the form of 'Leporello', for example), Heath-Stubbs had achieved some of his greatest successes.

I have given one long poem in its entirety – his debut, *Wounded Thammuz*. It deserves a much larger audience than it has so far found; for me it is one of the most important poems of the Second World War, capturing the mood of the autumn, winter and spring of 1940–41, the point at which the war seriously began to turn, where the genuine threat of a Nazi invasion of Britain became less pressing. After a long tiring slog, the poem insinuates, we will probably come through, and can begin the process of renewal and regrowth, but the dead will still be dead – their only hope is in the other, Christian myth cycle, of which Adonis and Thammuz (or Tammuz, a Sumerian counterpart of Adonis) are echoes. The context is plainest in the best lines of the poem, from section II of 'Spring Pastoral':

> So gaunt and sallow-visaged Spring came forth
> Across polluted Europe; uncouth paths
> Stalked he in green and firey slippers, spread
> His Eastern carpets over rubble-heaps,
> Pranked with the naked snowdrop, saffron-flower
> Of Colchis, Muslim tulip, mortuary
> Daffodil.

Wounded Thammuz is unmistakably a young man's poem. Its weaknesses are obvious: the archaisms, unevenness, detours into erudition, influences not quite digested. They are weaknesses we can afford to indulge. To call the poem charming would be to sell its ambition short, and yet it *is* charming, in a way that comparable early poems by Heath-Stubbs's contemporaries are not. Such lines as 'The moon's green blood in the mid-rib, and the rich red / Blood that is shed in the sunlight', are laughing off the risk of being laughed at, and display the kind of seriousness which puts at stake the possibility of silliness.

Many of the themes and images in *Wounded Thammuz* will reappear throughout Heath-Stubbs's work: the Christianity, the reworked mythology (my favourite in this vein is one of Heath-Stubbs's funniest poems, 'Not Being Oedipus'), the turn of the seasons. The unforgettable diving seabird, 'forked and arrowy', in *Wounded Thammuz*, is just the first of countless vivid birds (I have included the late collection *Birds Reconvened* almost in its entirety); and the poem as a whole is a kind of elegy, a form which he would, regrettably, have much recourse to. Two elegies for his undergraduate friends, 'The Divided Ways' for Sidney Keyes and 'Elegiac Stanzas' for William Bell, are among his most memorable work. The cosmology and angelology of *Wounded Thammuz*, deftly and enthusiastically handled, are medieval, borrowed from the lectures of C.S. Lewis, which he attended as an undergraduate in the early 40s. (Reading Lewis's *The Discarded Image* might be the best preparation for immersing oneself in Heath-Stubbs.) Oxford is itself a presence throughout Heath-Stubbs's poetry, as much as his beloved Soho and Fitzrovia; in the 'Elegiac Stanzas' the city itself participates in the working-out of grief, and in the long sonnet sequence 'The Heart's Forest', it forms a shadowy fourth partner in the bitter three-way relationship being described.

'What is ours of him,' he wrote of Keyes, 'must speak impartially for all the world.' I have taken this as an editorial maxim, going against his wishes in giving the poems as originally published (discarding changes made in the *Selected* and *Collected*), and in the order in which he published them. Furthermore I have included 'Epitaph', which he considered too anthologised, thereby running the risk of his curse against future reproducers. One decision gave me a lot of pause. I have not included anything from *Artorius* (1972). It is an astonishing long poem retelling the Arthurian legend, set up deliberately as a counterbalance to Charles Williams' *Taliessin through Logres*. It would be hard to call it a complete success; it changes tone too sharply, the satires on F.R. Leavis and contemporary feminism are out of place, when it describes boredom (as, again, in the satire on Leavis) it is itself boring. But without doubt it runs those risks of embarrassment that Heath-Stubbs had forbidden himself aged thirty ('a year in which, not I trust without irony, I composed my own epitaph, and proceeded to the formation of what I hope is a more mature and more intellectually disciplined style'). It was too long to include entire, and impossible to excerpt without misrepresenting.

The Text

The poems are given in the text of their first book publication. Most of the changes between these texts and those in the *Selected* and *Collected* are minor. In the 1965 *Selected*, the poems printed in 1945, 1946 and 1954 as 'Leporello', 'Don Juan Muses' and 'Donna Elvira' were gathered into a single poem called 'The Don Juan Triptych', and 'Valse Oubliée' was retitled 'Tschaikowskian Poem'.

Conventions for quotation marks varied among Heath-Stubbs's publishers. I have used single quotation marks throughout.

Something has gone wrong with the text of *Wounded Thammuz*: 'Spring Pastoral', section VI, lines 4–6, seem to have been garbled. Possibly a whole line is missing; omitting 'are' (or adding 'that') to line 6 makes some sense but warps the metre. I have let the garbled sentence stand. The manuscript of *Wounded Thammuz*, which might have provided an authoritative correction, is regrettably not among the collections of Heath-Stubbs's papers at the University of Leeds or the John Rylands University of Manchester Library.

Acknowledgements

Thank you to Bernard Saint, Henry King and James Keery, for their helpful suggestions; to the staff at Peter Ellis Bookshop, the Poetry Library, and the John Rylands Library in Manchester, for tracking down fugitive volumes; to my mother, for all her help with the text; and to my grandfather, Donald Rooum, for introducing me to Heath-Stubbs' poetry.

John Clegg

Selected Poems

Leporello

Do you see that old man over there? – He was once a gentleman's
  gentleman;
His skull is bald and wrinkled like a leathery snake's egg;
His forehead is not high, but his eyes, though horny, are cunning,
Like an old jackdaw's beginning to moult a few grey feathers;
His nose is sharp like a weasel's, and his lips always a little smiling,
His narrow shoulders crouched forward, hinting a half-finished
  bow.
Did you notice how beautifully white and smooth and soft his
  hands were?
His coat is dowdy as the dusty shards of a house-haunting beetle,
His cuffs and collar not quite white, like foam on a fouled mill-race.
But Fear flickers over his face – now settling like a fly
On his sunken cheeks, now haunting his blurred eyes;
And his pale mouth is always ready to fall open and gasp and
  shriek....
        Night after night he's here, in all weathers,
Drinking. They say his wife is a shrew and holds her head high
For all that once.... Night after night, under the yellow lantern-
  light,
Always the same old chair in the corner, night after night.
        But he likes to talk to a stranger – it makes a nice change.
Why don't you buy him a drink and get him talking?
        He can remember his master well – those were the days! –
Feast days, Carnival days – fans and flowers and bright silk shawls
Tossing like a poppy-patched cornfield the wind dishevels,
And then milky moonlight flowing over close-kept courtyards;
And while his master climbed the balcony, he would keep watch,
Whistle and rub his hands and gaze at the stars –
His co-panders; or there were mandolins murmuring
Lies under windows that winked and slyly slid open;
Or the hand's clutch and half-humorous gasp of the escapade,
And after a doubling hare's turn, choked laughter at fooled footsteps
Trotting away down wrong turnings; or when cornered
The sardonic, simple, decided flash of a sword – his master's sword.

And he can remember that night when he stood on the terrace
Sunning himself in black beams of vicarious sin,
While the waltz whispered within,
And three unaccountable late-comers came,
And gave no name –
(But she in the blue brocade is Anna:
And she has forged her outraged chastity into a blade
Of thin sharp ice-coloured steel; her hair is brown
And her eyebrows arched and black like two leaping salmon
Seen against the sun-flecked foam of a weir down-rushing;
And like a slim white hound unleashed she snuffs for the blood
Of a father's killer. And not far away is Elvira:
She wears silver and black and is heavily veiled
And has laid a huge jewelled crucifix over her hungry heart
In vain; for she is like an old frosty-feathered gyrfalcon,
With chrysolite eyes, mewed-up now, whose inactive perch
Frets her hooked feet; who cannot bear to gaze out
At the blue sky-paths slashed by young curving wings;
Her heart is a ruined tower from which snake-ivy
Creeps, fit to drag down an oak and smother him in dark green
    leaves.)
But the windows were all golden-spotted with candles,
Shadowed by dancing shapes; till above the silken strings
Flute and violin had trailed across the evening – a cry:
Zerlina, like a wounded hare tangled in that black net.

It is very quiet in the graveyard – a strange place to be waiting for
    him;
The moonlight hints queer perjuries – for all the Dead
Are tucked up snug in mud; we have heaped vast lumps of masonry
Over their head and feet, fenced them round with crosses
And stones scrawled over with white lies; we have given them
    flowers
Against the stench, and stopped their nostrils with mud;
We have lighted candles for hollow sockets; they will not trouble us;
They cannot see to climb the slippery stairs of their vault;
They are blind spectators who have long dropped out of the game –
But what if they didn't play fair? What if cold stone

Should speak, and offer unwanted advice? What if quite suddenly
This polished transparently reasonable world were shattered?
When the soft curtain of the night is ripped up by the bray of
  trombones,
And a dumb stone abstraction can speak, and the madman invites
  it to supper –
That is no laughing matter. If you are young and well-born
And have no heart, it seems you can go home and laugh,
Drink wine and do yourself well; but he, Leporello,
A poor man, sir, always attentive to business, no great scholar,
Had never thought of these things, didn't know how to deal with
  the dead gentleman,
Or Hell stretching out a flaming hungry arm
To snatch the ripe fruit of sin from the lighted banqueting hall.

      So that is why he has always a startled look, that old man;
For he feels he is being watched by dead eyes from behind the
  curtains,
And is still expecting a knock at the door, and the stone foot's
  tramp on the stairs.

Illusion

Wrapped in a velvet-soft piece of calf-skin,
With thoughts pressed between thin translucent sheets of India
  paper,
A volume of Emerson's Essays lies on the drawing-room table –
Rich, red, polished table, mahogany, red like old sherry,
Poised on its four slender feet with their carved lion-claws,
And the little book carelessly reclining there, carefully dusted
  daily.
  Sometimes the shy stranger in an absent moment
Nervously ruffled the white leaves, turning to the title-page:
There is Emerson's portrait; mild-browed and benevolent
He gazes serenely across the dim drawing-room.
  It is the primrose afterglow of a summer sunset;
The shadows begin to pace their pavane between the chair-legs,
(Oak and satin-wood, rose-wood and cherry-wood –
Trees from long-ago-felled forests are carved and fluted
Into shining curves and pillars). He cannot see to read
The flowery, starry hieroglyphics which the dark-eyed Persians
Have woven into the soft squares of the carpet.
Over there, the piano, huge, black, polished, three-legged monster
Grins with its ivory fangs agape. No longer
Waking are the ghosts that coiled round its wire
  heart-strings: –
Beethoven, Chopin, Brahms, Mozart and Mendelssohn.
  The windows have gazed out upon lawns and paths of golden
  gravel,
They have glimpsed the white-limbed to-and-fro-ness of tennis
  players dappling the vague heat-haze;
Children, moon-solemn and sun-haired, have drifted hand-in-
  hand between the borders,
They have heard the murmur of the mowing machine like the
  sound of a distant sea-surge,
And the call of blackbirds gilding again and again the edge of the
  evening...
  But the shy stranger, waiting there in the hushed drawing-room

Suddenly smiled, remembering it was all illusion:
A child's bubble-blown dream-palace, or perhaps this delicate
    chamber
Swam before the eyes of an old, half-blind witch-woman
Stirring the smoky embers of her dying turf-fire.
    He smiled when he remembered this; then all at once he felt
His naked feet sinking into deep drifts of dead leaves
And the cold thrusting-upwards of pale-stemmed toad-stools,
Saw again the dark shapes of the wet tree trunks around him;
Knew the air quivering with faint scents and stilled rustling
    sounds;
And over him, not very far above the tallest tree-tops,
Crouching, beast-like, the watchful, unfriendly sky.

Wounded Thammuz

> Thammuz...
> Whose annual wound, in Lebanon, allured
> The Syrian damsels to lament his fate,
> In amorous ditties, all a summer's day;
> While smooth Adonis from his native rock,
> Ran purple to the sea, supposed with blood
> Of Thammuz yearly wounded...
>
> Milton: *Paradise Lost*, Book I

1 AUTUMN RITE

I
Dull Time's unwinking sickle has close-clipped
My laurel boughs (Once more, and yet once more
Ye myrtles brown) and winter's cat's-tongue breeze
Has rasped away my roses, and has stripped
The quivering covering of my garden trees,
Hurling along the brown neap-tided shore
Autumnal discontent of unquiet seas.

And O you wind, as you come chattering
Between these broken strings, choke not my speech.
Break not this song, O break not this one song,
But bear about the winter-world some smattering
Of spring's shrill bird-bright runes, song-spells, and each
Flower-character inscribed my summer long.

This is that dying season when the Dead
Thicken the air, out of the still-born night
Wandering with yellow leaves, drifting with thin-
Spun webs of spider-silk; now should be said,
In the old way, for them, some litany, some rite.
I have no strength, but yet I will begin.

II

All the year's gold and silver is gone underground
     Into your cold dark caves, you fortunate Dead.
Helen and Cleopatra and all the crowned
     Queens of the ancient world lie low in that bed;
King Caesar has cast aside his sword and his diadem,
And Homer untuned his fiddle, to sleep with them.

It's time, oh it is high time, I should be lying
     Down in those shadowy fields where no wind blows;
In funeral garlands for me they will be tying
     With death-cold ivory fingers the deathless rose.
Up in this autumn world will the naked trees be mourning,
In twisted smoke from dank fires the old year burning.

III

A sieve of shell has sifted
The firstlings of the vine;
Are lifted on the pillar
Bunched grape and dangling bell –
Pom'granate, tendril-twine,
And golden-throated bell.

The barren sheaves are gilded
And swept towards the fire,
Are builded up for tinder;
Dry shells, autumnal leaves
Are pillowed for the pyre
Whose flames are scarlet leaves.

IV

This is the garden of the Dead –
Carved stone at each cold-pillowed head.
No dancing feet disturb the dew
Beneath the cypress and stiff yew,
Nor can the winds bend, as they pass,
The waxen lilies under glass.
Lichen and northward-thriving moss

In gold and velvet hide the Cross,
And angels by the unfruitful urn
Furl their broad marble wings and mourn
This is the place where fragrance fades –
Wasted ambrosia of shades;
Rosemary and remembrance die
On beds where sullied lilies lie.
How soon the freshest grass is cropped,
And the proud-turbaned tulip lopped,
The cockled ear of corn rejected,
The violet's sweetness neglected.
The crown-imperial droops and weeps,
While in his cave the Gardener sleeps.

V
Up on the high hill-tops and in their hollow caves,
Among rough rocks and raggedly-hewn crags,
Hard by the condor's eyrie and caverns of the cougar,
The centaurs dwell, those savage sagittaries,
With their shoulders unharnessed nor their trampling hooves shod –
But their broad brows are brother to the human.
They are leapers and laughers by the limpid cataracts,
Their moot the burnt-out crater, the crag and the crevasse.
With strong voice they shout to the strung shell of the tortoise,
Their corrugated trumpet the tragelaphe's curved horn;
They are harpers in the hollows of the unshadowy hills.
The wine of all their wisdom is the mead of the wild heather;
The light of the white-arched sky is still their lore and lust.
The shelves and the great ridges are their green grazing places;
They search out the salt-lick and fountains tinged with sulphur,
And they watch the dawn dancing over the dales and the steep
    cliffs
Reddening the stark stones and slopes all stippled with snow.
There is music in the mountains unmuffled by the nipping air
As they run with wild worship against the autumn wind.

VI

Bring fennel, and fresh parsley-garlands, and
The southern-scented vervain; bring carved bowls
    With maple-leaves entwined –
    Jaggéd and burned to gold;

Brim them with sweet new milk and stone-ground flour
Meddled with filmy must of sanguine wine,
    And honey, though the bees
    Now seek their torpid cells;

And bind your brows with ivy growing green
The winter through, and sharp bright apples from
    The rowan; range the white
    And crimson agaric

Around this dolmen-altar, older than
Delphos or Cumae or the Latmian hill
    Or Syrian gardens where
    Wounded Adonis sleeps.

Come you goat-footed dancers, shaggy-sided,
    Out of your panthered shades,
And you harsh-whinnying ones with the chestnut-shiny
    Flanks and swishing tails,
Trample our vintage with your heavy hooves
And rouse to uncouth din these old unechoing woods.

For we have sour and sweet glassy-cool clustering
    Grapes for the sore-parched mouth;
Our tangled hair hangs loose to the dappled fluttering
    Tags of a fawn-skin clout.
Disturb the fallen leaves with cone-tipped staff
Where through the woods there winds our mazy dancing-path;

Where shoulder-high grows all the fire-fringed bracken,
     Or where the squirrel whisks,
Or green to needled ant-hills' turgid traffic
     The hobbling wood-sprite dips;
Away, white-flagged, the startled rabbit goes,
Out of her thorn-thatched bed leaps up the bouncing doe.

And wake we with our clamour Echoes pined
In their dry stony cells, with tambourine,
     Cymbals, and wavering shawms,
     And round-toned kettle-drum.

And you, harp-player, snap those withered bays
That bind your long wire strings, conduct our rout
     To valleys whose steep rocks
     Shall bellow back your song.

Now through the waters of this quiet lake
Trundle the sacred cart, whose axle-tree
     And slow-revolving wheels
     The lucent wave shall purge.

Eastward, O wine-stained charioteer, lead on
To empires swart with shade, whose kings shall doff
     Their diamond crowns to deck
Our maypole hung with bells.

VII
Aurora Borealis fills the sky,
Bohemian birds the woods, both signs of war
Or pestilence. And whirl and whirl and whirl
The eddying leaves – Herodias' daughter
At her eternal dancing. Over the waters
Of this unfathomed lake glides a canoe,
Spattered with war-paint, hung with scalps and skulls,
And mouldering finger-flesh clutches the paddles;
The helm is guided by a bony hand...
These are the vanguard; ground cannot contain them,

But corpses sprout like luminous mushroom-spawn
In dark damp cellars, and the heavens sag
With the dull weight of ghosts; and now you hear
From every wood and garden and cross-road
(Cold cradle of the blasphemous suicide)
The petulant and uncomfortable voices of the Dead.

'Oh Life, Life, Life! Why have you stolen our life? –
The moon's green blood in the mid-rib, and the rich red
Blood that is shed in the sunlight? Why must we
Be creeping back again to this damp dead world, slinking
Down by the howling chimney and snuffling keyhole, scaring
Only the nerve-sick and ignorant, seeking
The carelessly-minded child, the unwary sleeper
Who lies with his throat exposed?

'We were the wise and strong – but now only
Psalm-singing in stuffy rooms, the squab-like medium,
The joggling automatic-writer and the juggling crystal,
The dog-eared Tarot with its train of senseless images –
The Emperor, the Female Pope, the Fool, the Hanging Man,
And the Lightning-Struck Tower which is the House of God.

'We are that impatient rider of the sea-shore,
With Beauty across his saddle-bow; his marriage-chamber
Is dark in the earth, and many a fresh young bride
Has he brought thither – ah, but a cold bed
Have those Lenoras and rare Margarets.

'We are the surgeon whose frozen hands were lopped;
The envious brain under an acid sky
Worm-screwed among the clamorous machines.
We are the poet within whose honeyed mouth
The ants have built their citadel. We are the patriot
Without a country; all tormented prisoners;
Lamia the child-devourer; the murdered usurer
Into whose poky cottage the young men broke
One night of curses, and spilt his lovingly-garnered

Gold-seeds of power on wine and trumpery women.
We are the shadow out of the broken mirror;
The burglar under the bed or in the cupboard.
We are the rats in the cellar. With our long nails
We'll undermine your palaces; with them
Is timbered Hell's ship she at last shall launch,
Pledged to destroy the world.'

VIII
A voice as of the wind, a Voice out of the Whirlwind:
'I am the Wild Huntsman, the wanderer of these mountains,
A whining among the wood, the word of the waving fir-tree;
I have wound the wounds of the sunset round with a winding
    cloud-wrack,
And you, wan things, are my quarry, as withered leaves to the wind.
My path is over the mountains, beyond the watchfires
And the blazing beacons of the clangorous marchmen;
By moors and mosses where no shepherd shoves
His sturdily-shod staff; by pinnacles
That turn the eagle dizzy and dislodge
The antelope, sure-footed ballador;
Up where the patient glacier-goddess drags
Her plough of glass; by frozen caves
Where cherubim their dreaming hermits cheer
With fire whose coal is more than diamonds.
O cower you down in your small burial-mounds? –
My thundering hooves shall break your earth-dome in,
Scatter your singing shin-bones, and shall mock
The ridged and rigid smile of the skull.
My ravens, Thought and Memory, shall pluck off
The golden bracelet from your fleshless arm,
The pearls which were your eyes. Oh withered leaf
That restless hang upon a restless tree,
Let the wind take you, and be lifted up
Into his own importunate energy!
And you, wild goats of the mountains, and goat-footed
Men, you horse-hooved dancers of the hills,
More madly urge your measure, frenzied be,

With the world's wine made drunk, and with the music
Of my inordinate pursuit; for I will drive you
To fields fenced round with lightning, and at last
Into my unimaginable folds.'

IX
'Southward, O wind, seeking the trellised vine,
Long has the fickle-pinioned swallow flown,
To amethystine clusters; but your breath,
Though nursing next year's seeds, rudely shall pine
Those birds who salt with song your bitter teeth,
Shall snuff the orange crocus-flambeau, blown
Too soon in mouths of all-tempestuous death.'

So sang the poet, softly, by the hearth
Of an old house, with embers raked together,
Warming himself by that uncertain glow,
(He who had served proud kings of the old earth –
But their bright livery was all for show,
And pitiful against the winter weather)
Then rose, and went on through the quiet snow.

2 MIDWINTER VALLEY

I
In a long midwinter valley of dry snow
The sphered and cavernous skulls by two by two
Lying. But in that sleep of death
What dreams may come? What images
Trouble the eyeless socket, haunt
This stony scaffolding? What thoughts revisit
The swept and garnished chambers of the skull?
                                        Only the wind,
Incessantly breathing over the chalk-white bones
With a high thin whizzing sound – as among sand-dunes
Siliceous windlestraw all night and day
Is pan-piped by an unempassioned breeze

While overhead a forked and arrowy bird
Plunges for glittering fish in glaring seas.

II
Then cold and hot and moist and dry –
Colourless mote-minuet within those cloistral spaces,
Echoes of stringless harps, and tetrachords
Invented by old gold Time's unstained centaur –
Steadfast, my eyeless friends, behold in sleep
The still blue flame within its cone of ice,
The pyramid among the flaring sands that stands
And looms and glooms under monotonous sun;
But you, Intelligences,
O tenuous-handed ones that twist and twine
A rope of twinkling pearls about the brain
That disembowelled squats within its empty chamber,
Whose hands and lips and – ah, bird-poignant feet
Strike out no fire, no sparks along the nerve
But wind in formal dance like the thistledown –
(With down upon your feet, ye nights and days!)
All with high movement of the seeds of things,
You circling ministers of crystal snow-dust
And all prismatic artifice of frost
Shake your frail sistra through our unwaked dream;
Then cold and hot and moist and dry –
Thin tunings of a twilight orchestra,
A rustling of primaeval fifths and octaves,
Tightening of strings and titterings through the air –
Not yet the angels move with shifting feet
Over God's polished floor in high pavane
Trailing their lace-like wings on bright mosaics
Inscribed with pentagons are still unread,
What time the trumpet shall be heard,
And rattling bones together fly
And Music shall untune the sky.

III

High up above my head I heard the golden plover's
Unearthly fluting, standing in a sad estuary
Where tufted lugworms bubbled, broken shells
Littered the muddy runnels. Bird, O bird,
O wisp of flesh and feather, web and mesh,
Unstaunched and inarticulate desire! Oh, and whither,
Threading these mists and miserable shores,
Treading these lone sea-beaches, and where tending,
Frail and tenacious one? Oh, without ending
The fumbling of numb waters with the sand,
While restless winter combs these bad sea-reaches.

IV

O can you not suspend
Your swift and singing spheres?
You bird-eyed stars unbind your glittering shoes,
Leave silent and untrod
God's sombre dancing-floor,
And cluster like ripe fruit in our damp woods.
But they shrill on, trembling like bright wine-glasses,
Nor yet the darkness passes.

Can you not soar so high,
You star-aspiring birds,
To build and breed in those moon-laden boughs?
You sharp-browed phoenix-clan
Climb through alternate skies
Of fire and snow to reach those radiant fields.
But Earth still has her fowling-nets to tighten,
Nor can the long night lighten.

V

And still the stream flowed on
Through the embowering darkness, a glittering
Great ring of glow-worm milk, trembling and swirled
By moonlight-bellied violins, a dance
Of swansdown, whirling with noiseless feet

Over a water-smooth, sedge-mirroring floor.
Below that music wooden puppets jerked,
Snapped their sharp fingers, mouthed with painted face –
And no light glinted on the spider-wires
That strung those jointy sockets, tenuous woof
Spun through and through the shrill Æolian air
Where quivering music shadowed voiceless dreams –
Thoughts of a dead man naked of his flesh
In blank midwinter valleys of the mind.

3 Spring Pastoral

I
Over the crumpled jaw-bones of the deep
All the long night, blowing the sharp salt spray
Inland, snapping the unglued chestnut-bud,
Howled the infuriate wind, rousing from sleep
Snow-sliding mountains, sending far astray
The homeward birds bewildered to the steep
Where shocked by the foul blast a lighthouse stood,
Till weary morning watched the grey tides creep.

Spring's cradle rudely rocked and heralded
By clarion storm out of the dank South-West;
The pale fruit-blossom shivered from the tree,
And young leaves mingled with the last year's dead;
Builds the undaunted thrush his mud-lined nest,
Shouting defiance from his bridal-bed
While wet winds raked along the grumbling sea.

II
So gaunt and sallow-visaged Spring came forth
Across polluted Europe; uncouth paths
Stalked he in green and firey slippers, spread
His Eastern carpets over rubble-heaps,
Pranked with the naked snowdrop, saffron-flower
Of Colchis, Muslim tulip, mortuary

Daffodil. Men marked with hungry eyes
In those Armenian and Sabaean mats
Embroidered pictures of forgotten lust.
But squint-eyed Spring
Squatted, prepared to haggle. Through the woods –
The old, the savage, devastated woods –
Was heard the mad and mocking cuckoo's cry.

III
Come in the early morning, Shepherds, bring
     Your tufted willow-wands,
Long hazel-catkins, and new-garnished knots
Clipped from the fresh-leaved hawthorn tree, and all
     The season's flowers.

Now the lush woods weep pools of hyacinth,
     And green primroses fade
Around the roots of venerable trees
And mossy banks where all the winter through
     They skulked unseen.

Bring these, and bring pert-flowering daisies, and
     The small blue violet,
The star-limbed celandine, and sanguine-tongued
Anemones wind-tottering, to this
     Dark woodland bier.

For now is time to lay in ground those limbs,
     Those towzled trampling feet,
And brows, grown hoary-fronted, with high horns,
Red lips that curled to many an ancient tune,
     Bright listening eyes.

Carry him down with songs and pipe-playing,
     Nor let the birds be mute –
But now in all their fresh spring plumage mourn;
They knew him well, and to his pastoral flute
     Made shrill reply.

Who knows, as round about his turf-built tomb
  We wind with mournful tread,
What shadowy feet shall echo as we dance
Our sad funereal measure, what cool hands
  Shall smooth our flowers?

But nevermore, you shepherds, nevermore
  Shall his pipe cheer your hills;
Your folds his watch, the shearing-feast his song
Shall lack, and these green lawns shall know
  His tread no more.

Nymphs and Shepherds, dance no more....

IV

Iron vineyards, stables for the fire-drake,
Forges, and mills, and wombs of molten metal,
Where rattling wheels together fly
As though they would untune the sky,
And men with sweaty faces walking among those fires...
They bring last year's corn, and coal, and diamonds –
Fodder for those great beasts; those which half-human
Champ like centaurs, with their shining steel flanks,
In their splendid pride and insolent lust of creation
Singing.
Some stretch forth, iron-pinioned demiurges,
Over a fiery chaos their measuring rods.
Others with delicate organs, fan-like antennae,
Intricate as hares' eyes, electric ears to catch
The inconceivable music of atomic dancing...
And these with shining hands
Have wrenched all our life's roots eternally awry.
Yet with magnificent plunging, let us set out to make
Tall towers our children, and plant blazing gardens
New-dight with quickfire and the steel-frost beauty
Of all the thick-set orchards of the sky.
Though nailed down
Under a leaden coffin-lid, stir ourselves to create,

Driving with a fearless ship through forward complexities,
Nor regretting the frail grace of our begetting.
For there is no turning backwards, and if need be, you must thrust
Your hardening man's face through fire-sleet desolation.
And so shall our maimed hero climb to his wry-faced throne.

V

My Love is over the sea to Spain
      And it's blow, you South Wind, blow!
And he'll bring me a pair of scarlet slippers
      That I to church may go.

My Love has sailed for Mexique Bay,
      And it's come, you ship, to land!
And he will bring me a golden ring
      To deck my lily hand.

My Love is gone into Muscovy,
      And it's oh, that he were sped!
And he'll bring me a pair of silken sheets
      Are sewn for our marriage bed.

Last summer we walked in the garden
      And the flowers they were never so bright.
'But heavy shall be the evening dew
      And your roses be withered tonight!

'Your roses shall wither tonight, my dear,
      But they will all be in flower
When I have sailed back over the water
      And come again to your bower.'

My roses are red, they are all full-blown,
      And my garden is gay to see,
The swallow has builded beneath the beam,
      But my Love comes not to me!

And I'd sooner the waters were turned to blood
    And I drowned under that sea
Than I should live to another spring
    And my Love proved false to me!

VI

What is this, dark against the setting sun?
A crooked tree, a vine whose iron tendrils
Are twisted to toothed wheels, and snake-sheathed chains,
And for fruit, a man hanging. This is the Vine-tender
Who clambered to his spring-time throne to curb
And gather grapes are full of blood. Even the wind
That howls so sharply and is twisted sore
Among those metal branches, is the shadow –
The moving shadow of a shifting star-dance
In his heroic halls.

Out of a silver wood
That waves above the mountain's silver-birches,
A bird has come, with strange sweet speaking-voice,
To sing imprisoned in our tarnished roses
Whose leaves are blood, whose thorns are iron nails.

This way turn, you women weeping
In the Temple porch, or by the little brook
That runs blood-red with the red earth of the hillside,
This way turn. And you who scour the mountains
Seeking in cool dark woods the boar-marred beauty,
Look here and see your ship-compelling Lover.

Long-lorn, forlorn tree, worn by Adam's serpent,
You bent and bowed, embraced by the meek Hero,
And the world groaned, where writhed your ancient roots.
But now your new leaves shake as the Spring wind
Disturbs the whispering souls that nest between
Crying of Southern gardens and of spices
Which tall flower-censers lift to clearer skies,
Lilies of fire, song of untaloned birds...
O Wind, break not my song!...

VII

Through skies as sweet as milk, and over grass
Tufted with velvet glumes, and whispering
Of sunlight-promise in the morning's mouth,
By tumbling seas gayer than painted glass,
By warm and naked hills, and over uncouth
Crags where rising birds gossip of spring,
Return, winged breezes dancing from the South!

Soft wind, come you, and blow away the rime
Of winter from the leaves, and fan to flame
Of flowers each slender fruit-tree branch, and rouse
New birds to song, now at the young year's prime.
Fresh wind, prevail, so shall you put to shame
Death; Spring wind, so shall you conquer time
Whose sickle has close-clipped my laurel boughs.

Mozart

Mozart walking in the garden,
Tormented beside cool waters,
Remembered the empty-headed girl,
And the surly porters,

The singing bird in the snuff-box,
And the clown's comic nose;
And scattered the thin blue petals
Of a steel rose.

An Heroic Epistle

From William Congreve to Anne Bracegirdle
circa 1729

Now it has all gone black, you are more than ever
The cadence of a voice to me, the turn of a prose phrase;
For my words in your mouth were a movement in time,
Like your hand's movement suddenly spreading the white
Fan, your turned wrist twisting the air;
Or the curve of your white neck, caught in a slant-light,
The tilt of your chin, and your smile mocking, mocking –
And then your laughter – and so your voice again.
     And never, my dear, was proud man's tenderness
Like this, never such patience;
A love not like a boy's love, nor a man loving like a boy, but rather
As one who has perfected some instrument
Of calculation – crystal, and chased gold,
And swinging steel, and mirrors set aslant
To each refraction of the sun's bright rays –
As such a man, long days in a dark workshop,
Brings forth this cold child of his quiet brain,
And after with delight knows all its rhythms,
The moods of its clear bright body –
Such was my love for you – the poet
Breathing his words into your silver throat,
Knowing each grace of your tongue, each turn of your hand,
Your musical body, so much more apt to movement,
Thus and thus, than mine, a man's, hard-thewed –
Yes, even the bright mysteries of your woman's body,
More than mere lover dares know – in the clear hard brain.
     But that was many years ago, in another century,
When love was still a ladder, and the brain,
The burning wit, crowned all the body's dancing.
Then was it thought crossing thought as the hand the hand –
At the point of contact, pleasure, at the intersection
Of wits, the laughter....

And at the turn of time our music reached
Its fulness, as a conceived child,
Closed in the female body, knows its time –
That play was my crown of myrtle, fillet of laughter,
My gift to you, and yours to me, and ours to the world –
And spurned by the world; but I have done with the world.
    And also in that year
John Dryden died, that great builder in words,
Poor and dislaurelled. They say that at his burying
Were strange things done; and it were something meet
That old man's corpse was carried off with laughter
Of fools, intoxication
(Which in the ancient times was of the gods)
Though only of fools.
    And so that age passed with him.
And now we live in a rounded time, rounded
With a low horizon of feeling until men break it.
We have forgotten the old high modes of loving,
And the song's poise is gone.
The intellect squats twisted like a spider,
A tortured, hunch-backed poet; or lurks, exiled,
Westward, within a starved and savage country –
(He will die mad.) There is the Duchess too,
Who will have an ivory image made when I am gone,
To sit at her table, smile, and nod its head –
But the laughter is gone, and youth is gone, and you
Are gone to pray.
You cannot make of me a saint, nor I
Of you a sinner – but the pride of wit
Is whittled down, and our long battle now
Lacks auditors, lacks point.
The fire is gone – we may find tenderness,
From each to each, uncomplicate, at last –
An actress who has left the Stage behind,
An old blind gentleman who once wrote plays.

Valse Oubliée

And as we came down by the staircase –
Broad the balustrade, shining and bronze in the lustre
Of hanging lights, smooth and strong to the touch like your arm –
Down the grand sweep of the staircase eagerly stepping,
We two, to the lighted ballroom, the swirl of my music,
You paused and said: 'The moon is a strange questing
Creature embodied out over these white plains –
But whether hunter or huntress, I do not know –
But whether hunter or hunted!'
And your mouth smiled, though while your eyes were thoughtful.
I said: 'She is a maiden pursuing, or a wild white falcon
Unmewed through the skies, or she is a hind, or a hound,
Or a frightened hare – the bewitched princess who wanders
There through the snow-covered night and over the pine-trees,
Or a wild swan perhaps, or a wizened dwarf,
Back-crook'd and broken because of his burden of silver,
Who stumbles home in the cold to his cave in the mountains!
But let us go down now to the lighted ballroom
Where they are expecting us, for the dance begins.'
And we went down into the hall, alone no longer.

    And standing by a window a girl said:
'Only once I saw one, once, once;
Far out over the snow, in a hard winter –
When I was a little girl, at our country place.
And Anya, our old nurse, said: 'Look, child –
Come to the window, and I will show you a wolf.'
(For often the long evenings she had told us of them)
And there it went, the lonely one, like a great dog –
But hindquarters narrow and drooping, like a cowardly dog –
Hungry nose to the snow, onward, onward.
But sometimes it paused, and scraped in its tracks, and raised
Its great head to the bitter skies, and howled.'

Oh curved, curved in a scroll the violin's neck and carved
With concentration of the patient hand;
And tight those strings and quick to break in the harsh
Air, and in the inclement weather;
And shrill, shrill the song of the strings, when the horse-hair sweeps
Caressingly upon them. And the flutes ice-blue, and the harps
Like melting frost, and the trumpet marching, marching
Like fire above them, like fire through the frozen pine-trees.
And the dancers came, swirling, swirling past me –
Plume and swansdown waving, white plume over golden hair,
Arms held gallantly, and silk talking – and an eye caught
In the candle-shadow, and the curve of a mouth
Going home to my heart (the folly of it!), going home to my heart!

And the black-browed girl by the window said, remembering:
'Always in my dreams it is thus, always in my dreams –
Snow and moonlight, snow and the dark pines moaning,
Fur over my body, and my feet small,
Delicate and swift to run through the powdery snow;
And my sharp mouth to the ground, hungry, hungry,
And always onward, onward, alone, alone...'

Moon, moon, cold mouth over the pine-trees,
Or are you hunting me, or I pursuing?

The Heart's Forest

1
(From Petrarch)

Now all alone and full of thoughts I go
  Through solitary fields, with my eyes fixed,
  Avoiding print of human foot, or any
  Trace of it upon the bare earth stamped.

There is no other remedy, there is
  No right way people's searching gaze to shun;
  For stripped I am of happiness, and thus
  Outward they mark how much I burn within.

Indeed, I think that every hill I climb,
  River or wood which I pass by, has found
  Out of my life's temper; else it were concealed.

And yet, however rough, however wild,
  The road I tread, Love comes there, close at hand,
  Still reasoning with me; and I with him.

2

The heart pauses and stands at gaze
  As you come through the forest of my soul,
  Seeking only your image in the pool
  Of laughter, and the wild rose;

The old grey wolf of lust
  That still pursued it, stops with dripping fangs,
  Powerless to rend; and folding her bright wings
  The eagle-intellect perches, disgraced.

And you, without concern,
   (Like the crazed Orfeo seeking his lost bride –
   His hair and beard grown like the lichen of trees)

Pass on under the branches, nor discern,
   Starring six times the shadows of the glade,
   Con-centrate on your face, their startled eyes.

3
Addison's Walk

Grove, and you trees, by careless birds
   Frequented, and you fronds, impersonal
   Whose greenness soothed the long intestine broil
   Within my head, when I would seek your shades

Those former months of solitude, remembering
   That sane cool mind who christened you, quietly
   In his discreet and formal century
   Beside the unhurried river's marge walking;

Now that together in the season's prime
   We've come this way, marked the symbolic flowers,
   And the axe striking on the murdered willows,

When this is over, and the wing of time
   Has brushed aside desire, in after years
   Returning here, what ghosts will haunt these shadows?

4

Leander gazed across the cold divide
   Of waters where, befogged, tall Sestos, dim
   With a hung light, mocking his absence, towered,
   Yet scrupled not to strip and plunge and swim:

Daring the monstrous people of the deep
    To impede his course; the still more monstrous loves
    Of sea-gods, who would drag him down to keep
    Him prisoner among their coral groves.

And I sit here with you in a yellow room
    Full of warm light and discourse, yet
    More deep and cold between us Dardan's sound;

For I shall never dare, with pliant arm,
    To dash those waves, negotiate that strait;
    And yet already I lie there, drowned, drowned.

5

In Winter, in a winter season of war,
    I turned from the Eastern gate where the iron men
    Sang their long chant of pain
    And let Love rattle his dice in my dry heart's core.

Now Spring returns, and now once more
    The flowers are out; the small birds sing again
    More meaningly than when I was alone,
    But I'm no nearer staunching my desire;

And Summer's end, or sooner, bids us part,
    And even by then, perhaps, wanting will be
    Banked down, and ready to sink like a child to sleep.

Yet I'll be wholly grateful for the art
    That all unknowing you have tutored me,
    Though Autumn bring me further cause to weep.

6

First Emblem: Dialogue of Mind and Heart

MIND:

Give over now, and let me be again
   A twisted thorn-tree shivering into flower,
   Beaconing the winds alone,
   With roots between the stones of an old tower.

HEART:

No, never more, for the soft woods are green,
   And I must go there, where I went before
   In dreams, seeking the vanished birds that plain,
   The nightingales that sing a backward year –

MIND:

Though Hope lies dead under the fallen leaves.
   The birds are flown, the axe is at the stock,
   A cold wind kills the buds as soon as blown.

HEART:

And there's no couch for lovers among graves,
   Nor singing when the treacherous lute-strings break,
   Nor climbing, brother, now the tower is down.

7

Three walked through the meadows in a forward
   Spring, and two were lovers;
   Supposing themselves one, needed no word.
   The third was tongue-tied: in his heart were hammers.

While these three paced the gaps in conversation –
   Lover and lovers – silent
   The third, and patient,
   Reviewing his unsatisfactory situation;

His hair and skin were dry as hay,
  His bones were clear like glass,
  The hammers in his heart were musical,

Breaking his tuneful heart, which still
  A damp cloth muted; but to the lonely walls
  At midnight in his room, spoke for all three.

8

The moon hangs over this city of the dead
  Fretting with silver walls which thought has worn,
  And each dark stone, proud and vocal as a swan,
  Sings, raising its head.

O Moon, my mistress, and O Death, my lover,
  Faithful in solitude, who tutored me
  In this old craft of song, oh do not be
  Jealous, now I forsake you for another;

But clothe my heart in silver and black for pride,
  Let it go dancing forth towards that cold
  Clear heart which it would win –

For oh, I would evade
  Before it is too late, your staled
  Virginity, O Death, and your cold kisses, Moon.

9

Since I am free, why do I linger here
  Among the shadows, while the impersonal train
  Stands ready to carry me from my despair,
  Shifting the mind's landscape with change of scene,

To that south country where the solitude
  Of field and forest can bring back again
  Only the sufferings of childhood
  When I was least troubled when most alone?

There, undisturbed by symbols I may watch
  Successive flowers, at April's end to catch
  The first notes of the tentative nightingale;

But yet I could not bear that this sharp love
  Should seem unreal; you, central now to life,
  Fade from the heart, because incredible.

10
'Fortunatus et ille deos qui novit agrestes'

'That man is favoured who has learnt to know'
  (The inscription says) 'the rustic deities.'
  The dove descants over the arching ways
  And the old cedar leans his long arms low;

And Time, a bird of passage, folds his wings
  To brood here, and the bells which call
  Out of the clock-towers lose their power to kill,
  While the quiet sun conducts the Spring.

It was the Roman, it was the tired
  Civil servant, who wore always
  His weary gown of duty, who desired
  The country godlings, and his villa's ease;

And I, debarred from your heart's garden ways,
Grateful to pause with you among these trees.

11

This night I walk through a forest in my head;
   In each tree's heart a lute, waiting the skill
   Of hand to chisel it, is musical,
   Already with a song stirring the glade;

All the hard wood cries to the stars that float
   Among the leaves, bird-sweet and shrill,
   Though no wires stretch nor delicate fingers mete
   Out their divisions, nor lute-master's skill,

And so, bewildered like one newly dead
   Who finds the myrtle-groves of Hades strange
   Country to him, I go among the trees

Seeking your image flickering through the shade,
   A madman's fire, and thus deluded range
   Cold hollows of my skull and echoing silences.

12
Second Emblem: Echo and Narcissus

ECHO:
I am a windy voice, voice to my voice
   Answering, within my stony cell,
   And pined for the dark boy over his pool
   Withdrawn, over the still mirror of glass

Which is his mind – oh never poacher hung
   More patient, tickling trout beneath the shade,
   As he to seize his naked beauty, with long
   White arms outstretched towards the flood.

NARCISSUS:
And if I trail my fingers in the cool
   Waters, or mar their smoothness, I displace
   The image I desire under the pool;

So I'll sit quiet here, until my face
    Is a white flower, and my blood green and still...

ECHO:
    But oh, I lie alone in the windy hill!

13

Blackbird, ironic on day's window-ledge,
    Full-throated chanter, sooty-plumed with pride,
    To hale me from my sterile crooked bed
    And the dream-haunted safety of night's cage

Into another day of wasted hope,
    Duty neglected, casual interviews
    Carefully staged, and pointing to a close
    Barren of ecstasy, and then to shape

(But oh, if favoured!) evening's conversation,
    Coil upon coil, and roads that always skirt
    The central meeting-place within the wood,

Because that heart is strange which has my heart,
    Because I came too late for consummation;
    O blackbird, blackbird, it isn't any good!

14

Now in my hall the rebel troopers stable
    Horses, whose iron hooves clang on the floor;
    They have hacked up to burn the great oak table,
    The wooden vine-leaves carved around the door;

And through my broken roof the waters beat,
    Beat, and the quick weather of sorrow falls,
    The rain coming down and mixed with withering sleet,
    Blurring the portraits and the storied walls.

And this cold wind and these black clouds that pelter
   Have overtaken us both in the dark wood,
   Were blowing up already in childhood,

And they have driven me back to that bare hall
   My heart – I have no other place at all;
   But you were wiser, going elsewhere for shelter.

15

Provençal singers, crying against the dawn,
   Whose symbol was the bitter nightingale,
   Seeking not Love's fulfilment but Love's pain,
   A darker resolution in the soul,

Sang with as strained and eager a voice as mine;
   But it is not their death-keeled dreams impel
   Me to imperfect modes to gain
   Solace of love, and bear down wit and will,

But my life's need; for like the married vine
   That dies when torn away from the elm's support,
   I cannot live for long, myself, alone;

Therefore, although indifferent, you will spare –
   Another love making lucid your quiet heart –
   The starved beast snuffling at its fastened door.

16
Third Emblem: Formal Invocation

Beautiful god, and terrible, with strong
   Bow at the shoulder hung, and at whose coming
   The Celtic swans wreathed Delos with a song,
   Close packed around that wandering isle, screaming;

You oracle-inspirer, whom
  The ordered dance delights,
  The white-robed choir with clear voice keeping time
  To measured cadence of the hollow flutes;

Think of the fleet-foot girl, who turned
  To cold dry bay-leaves in your outstretched hand,
  The overpowering scent of those crushed boughs;

Remember that dark boy, with drooping head
  And pain-struck eyes glazed, like a dying bird:
  Mindful of these, attend my suppliant voice.

17

Why to my writing finger I commit
  Words which as heavy hang
  As Charon's pennies on a dead man's tongue,
  Recording here a personal defeat,

While now, even now, under this clear March sky –
  And my friends' lives in pawn – two modes
  Of thought and being struggle on bitter roads
  (And the more scope for singing, so they say;)

I speak for those on whom this unjust time
  Has forced a solitude, whom chance
  And the machine defraud of any quiet;

And set in formal words' objective frame,
  Construct from my unhappy circumstance
  The microcosm of Europe's double heart.

18
Fourth Emblem: Hylas

I see plume-thistle and the violet
 Depending fingers of the long loosestrife,
 Meadowsweet, hemlock, formal silver-leaf,
 Nenuphar, and the crow-toe fingering it;

Then suddenly this quiet water is
 Cold laughter of a mouth which gathers me...
 My friend no longer by the cruel sea
 With desperate voice negates the silences.

The timeless prisoner of the inverted world,
 Unreal like these shadow-birds, is dumb
 As fish that cancel it, and oh, as cold:

You who prospect the sunset's golden wool,
 Beating to pulse of song the wild sea-foam,
 Think – my fate also is conceivable.

19

There is a hollow in my heart, a lost
 World, where never tardy breath
 Of Winter chills the hyacinth, nor frost
 Narcissus blank and beautiful as death;

There is a southern hollow on my heart's
 Bare mountains, and the birds which sing
 Among the branches, troublesome as thoughts,
 Shatter my sleep with memories of Spring;

And wandering all about these forest-shades,
 With long and fragrant hair unloosed to the wind
 And bosoms bare and torn, go women weeping –

Oh, in the Springtime! – seeking
   For all lost forms of love they may not find
   Where on the grass your wounded image bleeds.

20
Fifth Emblem: The Pot of Basil

THE SKULL:
You should have left me to the tender worm
   In the soft leaf-mould whittling away my eyes,
   Until some cold rain falling could erase
   Grief, and your brothers' crime;

But the pot cramps me, and the wild thyme
   Roots into my brain to recreate
   Those passionate thoughts should rot away with it,
   And spreads the air of death about your room.

ISABELLA:
But O my darling, though I know your heart
   Is hidden from me now, away in the deep
   Woods, nothing shall make us part;

For though I wake in the barren moonlight to weep
   I can be sure of you now as never I could
   Though your living body lay beside me in sleep.

21

Here in these woods where April is flamboyant,
   Birds drop their songs, each from his private tower;
   I mark the cuckoo's voice, inhuman, clear –
   Oh long expected vagrant! –

From the next field continually calling.
    So Spring's confirmed by her winged hierophant,
    And now's the time to pause and seek portent
    From those distinctive notes through the air trailing.

Particularly do I bear in mind
    How many singers and dead lovers heard
    Hope, guile or mockery in that chance crying;

And yet I fear it's now no way to find
    Conclusions for you, heart – not from a bird
    About his own peculiar business flying.

Don Juan Muses

over the dead body of the Commendatore

How beautiful, white and hard, are the teeth of this dead man –
The cold eyes fixed, and about the rigid mouth
The wrinkled lines of pain, like mountain canyons.
I have looked often upon the faces of the Dead,
And seen them carried with naked feet – bodies that had once been
Beautiful, obscure and draped in a plain coarse habit,
The stiff impersonal lines of Francis or Dominic –
To the cells of the grave, that always silent college.

And I remember the Day of the Dead; the offerings
Of flowers and fruit, and cakes set at their doors
By the country people, the hooded figures chanting,
And the many lights moving at noon in the sunlit square.

And now in the dark room, in the pause before
The blood is wiped from the blade, before the outcry
Begins, of the servants, and the woman's animal sobbing,
Before the scuffle in the street and the get-away,
I gaze on his cold face, where my own pride's image
Stares back at me – paternal body, stiff,
As though already he were turning to stone –
And so I wonder if this thing was not always
That which I most desired – oh, through the nights,
Those silver nights under a moon of summer,
When I carved my lust into song, or hid my face
In the dark forest of a woman's hair, or sought the comfort
And softness of their flesh; for pain deep-stemmed
Within the marrow, tension of the sinew,
Shall get no final comforting, until
I feel my living hand in a stone hand's clasp,
A stone man's eyes reflect my arrogance.

The Divided Ways

in memory of Sidney Keyes

He has gone down into the dark cellar
To talk with the bright-faced Spirit with silver hair;
But I shall never know what word was spoken there.

My friend is out of earshot. Our ways divided
Before we even knew we had missed each other.
For he advanced
Into a stony wilderness of the heart,
Under a hostile and red-clawed sun;
All that dry day, until the darkness fell,
I heard him going, and shouting among the canyons.
But I, struck backward from the eastern gate,
Had turned aside, obscure,
Beneath the unfriendly silence of the moon,
My long white fingers on a small carved lute.
There was a forest, and faces known in childhood
Rose unexpected from the mirrored pools;
The trees had hands to clutch my velvet shoulders,
And birds of fever sang among the branches;
Till the dark vine-boughs, breaking as I seized them,
And dripping blood, cried out with my own voice:
'I also have known thirst, and the wanderer's terror!...'

But I had lost my friend and the mountain paths;
And if there might have been another meeting –
The new sun rising in a different sky,
Having repaired his light in the streams of Ocean,
And the moon, white and maternal, going down
Over the hills – it is too late
Ever to find it now.

And though it was in May that the reptile guns
And breeze-fly bullets took my friend away,
It is no time to forge a delicate idyll
Of the young shepherd, stricken, prone among
The flowers of spring, heavy with morning dew,
And emblematic blood of dying gods;
Or that head pillowed on a wave's white fleece,
Softly drowning in a Celtic sea.
This was more harsh and meaningless than winter.

But now, at last, I dare avow my terror
Of the pale vampire by the cooling grate;
The enemy face that doubled every loved one;
My secret fear of him and his cold heroes;
The meaning of the dream
Which was so fraught with trouble for us both;
And how, through this long autumn
(Sick and tempestuous with another sorrow)
His spirit, vexed, fluttered among my thoughts,
A bird returning to the darkened window –
The hard-eyed albatross with scissor bill.
And I would ask his pardon for this weakness.

But he is gone where no hallooing voice
Nor beckoning hand can ever call him back;
And what is ours of him
Must speak impartially for all the world;
There is no personal word remains for me,
And I pretend to find no meaning here.
Though I might guess that other Singer's wisdom
Who saw in Death a dark immaculate flower,
And tenderness in every falling autumn,
This abstract music will not bring again
My friend to his warm room:
Inscrutable the darkness covers him.

Donna Elvira

That stone death walking the castle corridors,
Whose clanking tread rouses the foxes' bark
Overhead in the high sierra, under a darkened moon,
And sends an echo to these worn battlements; his eyes
Are hollows of the grave, full of blue candles,
Clefts in the mountain's granite, where bright riders,
Black-horsed, with streaming hair, dash to oblivion –
John, it is you he is looking for. He is your fear:
The solitary spectre
Who roars in the labyrinth's centre, in a low vault
Where naked and alone you fight in dreams,
And start from your lover's arms, under a light sheet,
Moaning in sleep, while she lies quiet as a sea
And morning's fingers twitch at the dead curtains.

That striding man in marble I, too, have seen,
Who have known you, as they have never known,
Those others, others: the ladies moving
In Moorish gardens, bright as roses, light as fountains
Falling in laughter between the tamarisk hedges,
Or muffled at mass with stars behind their veils,
For whom love was a dance on a glass floor,
Tricky, with peacock steps, or posturings
Of the white-tufted crane beside a sunset pool;
Who tripped and fell, poor dolls, their jointed limbs
Snapped in the tangled wires the puppet-master held.
Or the clustered nuns, murmuring like black bees
Home to their stone hive, in a white vigil;
Those virgins of the night, into whose dreams
You suddenly pranced, hot as a painted devil
Out of their picture-books; or simpering,
With your fake martyr's wounds, your sacred heart upon your sleeve,
Peeked from the saints' procession over the altar, soft-mouthed and meek
As any anatomical flayed Bartholomew
Or young Sebastian hedgehogged with arrows.

The peasant girls, gossiping by the fountain,
Or silly as their geese at noon under the cork-trees,
Giggle and shrink, seeing your riding shadow
Skim on the pasture, your tall high-stepping horse
Galloping back to the predatory castle
Perched on the crags like a harsh-feathered buzzard.
For them you are legendary as that long-nosed goblin
Who skulks by twilight underneath the eaves,
Or the green-toothed ogre in the Goth-king's grave,
Snoring amongst his gold, who every May-day night
Claims a plump virgin for his supper there.
But I was proud-born of a metalled race,
And as a girl I dreamed a duke or a prince
To be my only husband; or else, perhaps,
Married in a long black veil, to lie alone,
A grove of cedars, where only the white Dove
Might come, and brood, and build his secret nest.
But when I spoke of this, Pasquita, our old nurse,
Combing my long locks by the firelight, would laugh, and say:
'What, these to be shorn away! Lie cold, then, to the cold moon!
No, girl – but these are snares
To catch some wild lover – the bandit-king,
Who will make you rich from his gold-cave in the mountains,
And kidnapped countesses to be your waiting women;
Or the phantom huntsman who rides on windy nights
Over the hills, chasing the ghosts of kings.'

But once, in the market-place,
I peered between the curtains of my litter
And saw a gipsy-girl dancing among the crowd;
Flaunting like a flower her brown body, she fixed her eyes –
Eye of a gipsy, eye of a wolf –
Upon the man she wanted, and drew him forward,
Swaying her hips and arms, and her young breasts,
To the rhythm of castanets and clapping hands;
She seemed as ancient
As a goddess painted on a cave's flat wall
In red and yellow ochre; and beckoned him –

A tall young mule-driver – to love as to destruction.
Then my blood cried that I was one with her,
And one with the shifting moon, and the harsh sea,
And the hungry grave, the last of all your lovers.

You have pulled down my pride. There is none left;
And my dreams shrivel like rose-leaves in the fire.
I have run bare-foot up and down the streets
Like any raddled whore who's lost her swaggerer.
Your servant, too, has led me by the snout:
That little man, with a weasel's nose,
Who scans the dry anatomy of your desires,
And has cast-up, and ruled in his account-book
The profit and the loss of all your lust.
He knows you, too; therefore he, too,
Shall meet that stone death on the stairs, and live.

But now I am the black-faced moon that speaks to your ebb-tide;
The Banshee, with a night-bird's voice,
Trailing my veils of shade, boding of death.
Be free then from my love, whose whimpering muzzle
Follows your heel no more. Another hand
Arrests your fingers on the passionate sword-hilt.
At last you have been caught; put a bold face on it –
A dirty schoolboy breaking bounds at night –
But I was the night, and I the apple-tree.
How transient you are –
Poor lord, poor lover, less than a ghost,
Who have no flesh and blood but our desire.

To the Mermaid at Zennor

Half fish, half fallen angel, none of you
Human at all – cease your lust's
Cold and insatiate crying from the tangled bay;
Nor, sea-hag, here
Stretch webbed and skinny fingers for your prey.

This is a hideous and a wicked country,
Sloping to hateful sunsets and the end of time,
Hollow with mine-shafts, naked with granite, fanatic
With sorrow. Abortions of the past
Hop through these bogs; black-faced, the villagers
Remember burnings by the hewn stones.

Only the saints,
Drifting on oak-leaves over the Irish Sea,
To sing like pipits from their crannied cells
With a thin stream of praise; who hear the Jennifer
Sob for her sins in a purgatory of foam –
Only these holy men
Can send you slithering from the chancel steps,
And wriggling back to your sunken paradise
Among the hollow-eyed and the capsized.

A Charm Against the Toothache

Venerable Mother Toothache
Climb down from the white battlements,
Stop twisting in your yellow fingers
The fourfold rope of nerves;
And tomorrow I will give you a tot of whisky
To hold in your cupped hands,
A garland of anise-flowers,
And three cloves like nails.

And tell the attendant gnomes
It is time to knock off now,
To shoulder their little pick-axes,
Their cold-chisels and drills.
And you may mount by a silver ladder
Into the sky, to grind
In the cracked polished mortar
Of the hollow moon.

By the lapse of warm waters,
And the poppies nodding like red coals,
The paths on the granite mountain,
And the plantation of my dreams.

Address Not Known

So you are gone, and proved bad change, as we had always known,
And I am left lonely in London the metropolitan city,
Perhaps to twist this incident into a durable poem –
The lesson of those who give their love to phenomenal beauty.

I am coming to think now that all I have loved were shadows
Strayed up from a dead world, through a gap in a raped tomb,
Or where the narcissus battens in mythological meadows:
Your face was painted upon the coffin-lid from Fayoum.

Is this my pain that is speaking? The pain was not long protracted:
I make a statement, forgive the betrayal, the meanness, the theft.
Human, I cannot suppose you had planned all that was enacted:
Fortitude must be procured to encounter the hollowness left.

The sun will not haver in its course for the lack of you,
Nor the flowers fail in colour, nor the bird stint in its song.
Only the heart that wanted somehow to have opened up
Finds the frost in the day's air, and the nights which appear too long.

Elegiac Stanzas

in memory of William Bell

Fretful, with all her fine deceits of mind
About her still, and still unchanged, the city
Opens her grey heart to mild January,
With medlars and mortality in her hand;

Where in their windy towers the old men weep,
Remembering how soon the goddess fled
(Before they woke and found how youth was dead)
While she but touched their parted lips in sleep.

But I recall that Irish sorcerer –
His table set, the tall glasses of wine,
All Souls' tide summoning at the bell's last groan
His wandering shades to a thin-fumed banquet here –

Whose lonely ceremony I need not prove,
Since pausing at the end of every street,
Rustling homewards through these skies I greet
Poems, like birds, that seek the sacred grove.

But when the night is come, from their sublime
And baroque heavens the great musicians bend:
Sebastian Bach, eternity on his mind,
And Monteverdi, between the seraphim,

Yet whispering now with the year's gentlest breath –
'*Zefiro torna, torna...*' – whose complaint
Is formal landscapes and the nymph's lament,
And how Spring brought no solace for her grief.

Oxford, January 21st – 23rd, 1949

Epitaph

Mr Heath-Stubbs as you must understand
Came out of a gentleman's family in Staffordshire
Of as good blood as any in England
But he was wall-eyed and his legs too spare.

His elbows and finger-joints could bend more ways than one
And in frosty weather would creak audibly
As to delight his friends he would give demonstration
Which he might have done in public for a small fee.

Amongst the more learned persons of his time
Having had his schooling in the University of Oxford
In Anglo-Saxon Latin ornithology and crime
Yet after four years he was finally not preferred

Orthodox in beliefs as following the English Church
Barring some heresies he would have for recreation
Yet too often left these sound principles (as I am told) in the lurch
Being troubled with idleness, lechery, pride and dissipation.

In his youth he would compose poems in prose and verse
In a classical romantic manner which was pastoral
To which the best judges of the Age were not averse
And the public also but his profit was not financial.

Now having outlived his friends and most of his reputation
He is content to take his rest under these stones and grass
Not expecting but hoping that the Resurrection
Will not catch him unawares whenever it takes place.

The Last Watch of Empire

for Fred Marnau

The ultimate dream. Arms, eagles, broken banners,
And a blind battle in the naked wood.
Over the brazen birds
Those with black shining feathers that scream and tear;
The angels rending their bright hair
Amid the fog and babel of crying voices,
Where Cyril and Methodius snatch at their split hearts.

Look now, this
Is the last Emperor, whose crown of ice and gold
Drops diamonds like frozen tears, like those smooth stones
The glacier bears from mythological mountains.
Now he has fled into the forest, where
The elk and wild boar their yellowing bones
Abandon to the ghost-led traveller;
With his great hands, heavy with seals, he scratches
For acorns, beech-mast, against hibernation,
Through winters which no rising sun, no moon
Prompting the green unfolded bud, shall loosen,
In his gem-fiery chamber among the roots.
(Sleep Caesar, though the hunter's horn
Be still lamenting over your slate-grey head:
It is not time, not yet).
Till corn and roses rise from his brain, his heart.

The holy Malachi, in a western island, once
Prophesied this: the Roman Peter feeding
His flock amid great tribulations,
Destruction riding over the seven hills.
Now an old man, in a secret mountain cave,
Sits, with wax-white hands to bless, and hair
Light on the wind, and grey as cobwebs;
Where eleven hermits, as spry as wagtails, twitter,
Raising their spare throats to the dawn's cold beams.

St Luke's Summer

St Luke's Summer, the Silver Age of the year –
Chryselephantine autumn, white cloud and gold leaf
Recalling an ivory shoulder, the light in your hair –
Let the still rains drip to my heart, and rinse it of grief!

But is there any dabbing could expunge that stain?
Too well and too constant the Shadow has conned his brief
To indict this specious season a common thief,
Filching the warmth from the year, but leaving my pain.

The lackeys of Summer paid off, wood-wren and swallow
In a mythical and inaccessible Africa
Are hoarded and harboured now, where I may not follow.

That you, too, are absent proclaims each vapid evening;
Therefore I make my petition to great Verticordia,
And may love likewise come back with the seasons' returning.

The Unpredicted

The goddess Fortune be praised (on her toothed wheel
I have been mincemeat these several years)
Last night, for a whole night, the unpredictable
Lay in my arms, in a tender and unquiet rest –
(I perceived the irrelevance of my former tears) –
Lay, and at dawn departed. I rose and walked the streets,
Where a Whitsuntide wind blew fresh and blackbirds
Incontestably sang, and the people were beautiful.

A Ballad of Pope Joan

Joan she was an English girl
   Born at West Hartlepool;
Scotus Erigens taught her Greek
   When she sneaked in to school.

'From All to nothing creation goes'
   He said – '*O entium ens!*'
The scholarship-boys rose up like a man,
   Transfixed him with their pens.

Joan she sat with the curate at play:
   'Will ye gang, Lizzie Lindsey,' sang he
'Will ye gang to the hieland heights of Religion,
   Your petticoats up to your knee?'

'O I will follow my own true love
   In any weather or wind;
I will fly to the forests of Arden and Eden
   And my name is Rosalind.'

Fever, famine and fury of Northmen
   On the map of Europe crossed;
The people died like flies, only quicker,
   And the curate, somehow, got lost.

Joanna came to the city of Rome,
   Being discreet and highbrow,
And the shattered statue of Venus Genetrix
   Cocked an ironical eyebrow.

Oh who shall jangle St Peter's keys
   And mount the Pontifical throne?
This girlish-faced young monk, demure,
   And relatively unknown.

From *The Triumph of the Muse* (1958)

Solemn procession through the streets:
  'Bless us and pray for us,
Joannes sevus servorum Dei
  Pontifex maximus!'

Joan gazed up at the blank, blue heavens,
  And her heart was a puddle of fear;
'Alas I have that in my womb...' she muttered,
  For she knew her hour was near.

The seven Archangels before God's throne
  In their adamantine mail
Trembled: 'Oh Pillars, support your Church,
  Lest the gates of Hell prevail!'

Then the three Pillars of Peter's dome
  Gasped in their stony lungs,
And over all the astonished city
  Clattered their marble tongues.

And the first Pillar was craggy Cephas;
  'I haul at my net,' said he
'For haddock and mackerel, herring and dory,
  But there's queerer fish in this sea.

'My net is a tough and close-meshed net,
  And if any breaks through and goes,
I curse and swear in my Billingsgate...
  But then the red cock crows.'

And the second Pillar was James the Just,
  And he said: 'The accusing Law
Clutches at my Davidic heart
  With a cold and constricting claw!'

And the third Pillar was John, the thunderbird:
  'I have seen the Whore and her Snake
Rampaging over the Seven Hills
  To the incandescent lake.

'But my Love, the terrible brazen-footed
    Alphabet looks on me:
O adorable, ridiculous children
    Love one another,' said he.

Then Mary leaned from among the Angels,
    Observing Joan and her fear:
'There are times', she said, 'when a girl needs Mother,
    My dear, but ah my dear.'

Then Joan fell down in the public street,
    With the harsh cobbles for a bed:
And the taxis stood and hooted like furies,
    Till the crossing lamps turned blood-red.

And 'Oh, oh, oh,' cried Joan and 'oh,
    Assist me gentlemen please!'
Then the baby ripped itself from her womb,
    And addressed them in words like these:

'I am Long Will of Cumberland,
    And Will of Malvern Hill,
And Will of the Tyger and the Lamb,
    And Arden and Avon's Will.

'I voyaged to the Southern polar Seas,
    And Samson's blindness was mine,
And I twice rode pilgrim, to Canterbury
    To Thomas the Martyr's shrine.

'Immortality flies round my head,
    And urns and nightingales;
True Thomas I am of the Eildon Tree,
    And Taliesin of Wales.'

....

They buried Joan by the street-crossing,
With the baby at her feet,
And continually circumambulate
To avoid that scandalous street.

Not Being Oedipus

Not being Oedipus he did not question the Sphinx
Nor allow it to question him. He thought it expedient
To make friends and try to influence it.
In this he entirely succeeded,

And continued his journey to Thebes. The abominable thing
Now tame as a kitten (though he was not unaware
That its destructive claws were merely sheathed)
Lolloped along beside him –

To the consternation of the Reception Committee.
It posed a nice problem: he had certainly overcome
But not destroyed the creature – was he or was he not
Entitled to the hand of the Princess

Dowager Jocasta? Not being Oedipus
He saw it as a problem too. For frankly he was not
By natural instinct at all attracted to her.
The question was soon solved –

Solved itself, you might say; for while they argued,
The hungry Sphinx, which had not been fed all day,
Sneaked off unobserved, penetrated the royal apartments,
And softly consumed the lady.

So he ascended the important throne of Cadmus,
Beginning a distinguished and uneventful reign.
Celibate, he had nothing to fear from ambitious sons;
Although he was lonely at nights,

With only the Sphinx, curled up upon his eiderdown.
Its body exuded a sort of unearthly warmth
(Though in fact cold-blooded) but its capacity
For affection was strictly limited.

Granted, after his death it was inconsolable,
And froze into its own stone effigy
Upon his tomb. But this was self-love, really –
It felt it had failed in its mission.

While Thebes, by common consent of the people, adopted
His extremely liberal and reasonable constitution,
Which should have enshrined his name – but not being Oedipus,
It vanished from history, as from legend.

Lament for the 'Old Swan', Notting Hill Gate

The Old Swan has gone. They have widened the road.
A year ago they closed her, and she stood,
The neighbouring houses pulled down, suddenly revealed
In all her touching pretentiousness
Of turret and Gothic pinnacle, like
A stupid and ugly old woman
Unexpectedly struck to dignity by bereavement.

And now she has vanished. The gap elicits
A guarded sentiment. Enough bad poets
Have romanticized beer and pubs,
And those for whom the gimcrack enchantments
Of engraved glass, mahogany, plants in pots,
Were all laid out to please, were fugitives, doubtless,
Nightly self-immersed in a fake splendour.

Yet a Public House perhaps makes manifest also
The hidden City; implies its laws
Of tolerance, hierarchy, exchange.
Friends I remember there, enemies, acquaintances,
Some drabs and drunks, some bores and boors, and many
Indifferent and decent people. They will drink elsewhere.
Anonymous, it harboured
The dreadful, innocent martyrs
Of megalopolis – Christie or Heath.

Now that's finished with. And all the wide
And sober roads of the world walk sensibly onwards
Into the featureless future. But the white swans
That dipped and swam in each great lucid mirror
Remain in the mind only, remain as a lost symbol.

From *The Blue-Fly in his Head* (1959)

The History of the Flood

Bang Bang Bang
Said the nails in the Ark.

It's getting rather dark
Said the nails in the Ark.

For the rain is coming down
Said the nails in the Ark.

And you're all like to drown
Said the nails in the Ark.

Dark and black as sin
Said the nails in the Ark.

So won't you all come in
Said the nails in the Ark.

But only two by two
Said the nails in the Ark.

So they came in two by two,
The elephant, the kangaroo,
And the gnu,
And the tiny little shrew.

Then the birds
Flocked in like wingèd words:
Two racket-tailed motmots, two macaws,
Two nuthatches and two
Little bright robins.

And the reptiles: the gila monster, the slow-worm,
The green mamba, the cottonmoth and the alligator –
All squirmed in;

And after a very lengthy walk,
Two giant Galapagos tortoises.

And the insects in their hierarchies:
A queen ant, a king ant, a queen wasp, a king wasp,
A queen bee, a king bee,
And all the beetles, bugs, and mosquitoes,
Cascaded in like glittering, murmurous jewels.

But the fish had their wish;
For the rain came down.
People began to drown:
The wicked, the rich –
They gasped out bubbles of pure gold,
Which exhalations
Rose to the constellations.

So for forty days and forty nights
They were on the waste of waters
In those cramped quarters.
It was very dark, damp and lonely.
There was nothing to see, but only
The rain which continued to drop.
It did not stop.

So Noah sent forth a Raven. The raven said 'Kark!
I will not go back to the Ark.'
The raven was footloose,
He fed on the bodies of the rich –
Rich with vitamins and goo.
They had become bloated,
And everywhere they floated.
The raven's heart was black,
He did not come back.
It was not a nice thing to do:

Which is why the raven is a token of wrath,
And creaks like a rusty gate

When he crosses your path; and Fate
Will grant you no luck that day:
The raven is fey:
You were meant to have a scare.
Fortunately in England
The raven is rather rare.

Then Noah sent forth a dove
She did not want to rove.
She longed for her love –
The other turtle dove –
(For her no other dove!)
She brought back a twig from an olive-tree.
There is no more beautiful tree
Anywhere on the earth,
Even when it comes to birth
From six weeks under the sea.

She did not want to rove.
She wanted to take her rest,
And to build herself a nest
All in the olive grove.
She wanted to make love.
She thought that was the best.

The dove was not a rover;
So they knew that the rain was over.
Noah and his wife got out
(They had become rather stout)
And Japhet, Ham, and Shem.
(The same could be said of them.)
They looked up at the sky.
The earth was becoming dry.

Then the animals came ashore –
There were more of them than before:
There were two dogs and a litter of puppies;
There were a tom-cat and two tib-cats

And two litters of kittens – cats
Do not obey regulations;
And, as you might expect,
A quantity of rabbits.

God put a rainbow in the sky.
They wondered what it was for.
There had never been a rainbow before.
The rainbow was a sign;
It looked like a neon sign –
Seven colours arched in the skies:
What should it publicize?
They looked up with wondering eyes.

It advertises Mercy
Said the nails in the Ark.

Mercy Mercy Mercy
Said the nails in the Ark.

Our God is merciful
Said the nails in the Ark.

Merciful and gracious
Bang Bang Bang Bang.

Variation on a Theme by George Darley

It is not beauty I desire
    And not – but not – the virtuous mind:
Marks of potential tragedy –
    These stigmatize the human kind.

And lonely in the darkness, I
    Surmise your pain, your loneliness,
And stretch uneasy arms towards
    That inarticulate distress.

If sons and daughters of the gods
    Stride careless through the market-place
What can we but avert our eyes –
    Acknowledge, not demand, their grace?

Although the smooth olympian brow
    Bids Greece and Ilium beware,
More turbid tides on love's dark sea
    Involve us with the siren's hair.

Each hard-faced doctor who expounds
    Within the rigid schools avers
That God Himself loves His elect
    Yet for no merit that is theirs.

And, fuel to the appalling creed,
    By human analogues we know
We do not love the beautiful
    But, loved, they are imputed so.

Old Mobb

Old Mobb stood on the Romsey road:
A splendid equipage came along –
Inside was the Duchess of Portsmouth, with two French footmen,
And two sleek and pampered spaniels.
'Fellow,' she said, 'do you know who I am?'
'Yes, and what you are –
You are the king's whore, I think,
And not kind Protestant Nellie, neither.'
'Villain, do you dare to touch me there!'
'Now I command where the king asks his favours,'
Said Old Mobb, politely removing
Three hundred pounds, a little gold watch,
And a very splendid string of pearls.

2

Old Mobb was on the road at midnight:
Mercury, patron of thieves, swung in its orbit.
Came ambling by on an old grey mare
Mr John Gadbury the astrologer.
'I am a poor man, a poor scholar,
Pray you, spare me.' 'What you –
Who lease out the seven stars for hire
To cozen noodles. These golden chimers
And these silver chinkers make better music
Than all the circling spheres, and much more audible.'
Said Old Mobb, as he pocketed them.
'You cannot rob me of my skill,' said Gadbury,
'In physiognomy, and from your favour
I read you born for hanging.'

3
Came trotting along on a neat black pony
Dr Cornelius Tilburgh,
Successful physician, with a bedside manner,
'Have you no care,' said he, 'for those
Your depredations ruined?'
'You with your clysters and blisters, your nostrums and boluses
Ruin more men than the cataracts of the Nile.
Here, doctor, is a leaden pill –
Cough up, or void your superfluity:
No antidote, you know, for gunpowder.'
Said Old Mobb, as he extracted
Twenty-five pounds and a bright medal
With the king's own face upon it.

4
A proud coach rumbled along
On the road towards the Winchester Assizes.
Judge Jeffreys stuck his head out of the window –
His great full wig, his brazen blotchy face:
'The law has claws and I incorporate the law.
Don't think, my man, that you'll escape from justice.'
'Though I shall dance on Tyburn, and you
Rot in the Tower, awaiting trial –
Yet there's another Judge we both must go to.
Who will fare better at those final sessions –
The Lord Chief Justice of England, he who hanged
Many poor men of the West at their own doorposts,
And doomed Dame Alice for her mere compassion
To broken fugitives, or a plain man of Hampshire
Who knew no master but his poverty?
Though he brandished a gun he never killed any
And prayed often
For God's forgiveness, even while he robbed,
As now I do.' said Old Mobb
Suiting the prigging action to the word.

The Watchman's Flute

(Kano)

Through the Nigerian night the Tuareg watchman,
Ferociously armed with sword, daggers and whip,
Intermittently blows his flute – a piece of piping
Bored with five holes: to pass the time –

To ward off tedium, and perhaps
Lurking malignant ghosts that always throng
This ambient, African darkness:

Infinite rhythmical variations
On a simple tetrachord, with a recurrent pedal point –
Libyan music, antique – as Orpheus
Cajoled the powers of Hell, made them disgorge
Eurydice – to him she was love
(Her jurisdiction be wide).

Those deliquescent forms shrink back
To hollow pits of non-entity:
Music implies an order – light,
Particles in regular motion,
The first articulate Word.

May my lips likewise
Mould such melodious mouthfuls still, amid
The European, the twentieth-century tediums:
We too are haunted, we are in the dark.

Christus Natus Est

'*Christus natus est!*' – it was the Cock's carol
Into the darkness, prefiguring a betrayal.

'*Quando?*' – the Duck's call is harsh,
Sounding from the reeds of a desolate marsh.

'*In hac nocte.*' – that voice was the Raven's,
Boding into Man's castle the fatal entrance.

'*Ubi?*' – it was the Ox that spoke:
We kick against the pricks, we are under the yoke.

'*Bethlehem!*' – the lamb, kept for slaughter, said:
God has taken flesh in the House of Bread.

A Formality

In Memoriam T.S.E.

Poetry is a formality: a continual greeting and leave-taking
For all that we encounter between
A darkness and a darkness. Hail and farewell
To the seven-braided spectrum. At dawn, at sunset;
And each particular thing we learn to love
We must learn to do without. Celebrate this;
Poetry is a formality.

Poetry is a formality: with words we clothe
The naked abstract thought, shivering in its shame –
Only with leaves, only with coats of skin? We can do more –
Go brave through the infected winter
Of our condition. Carnival.
Mask yourself, then. Poetry
Is a formality.

Poetry is a formality: to each
His way of speaking. I would emulate those
Who countered despair with elegance, emptiness with a grace.
And one there is now to be valedicted
With requiem. Poetry also? Also poetry is
A formality.

The Scops Owl

On marble hills and glaucous olive leaves
Shadows begin to fall. Now the small, brown,
Staring, ear-tufted scops owl will begin
His curfew, his reiterated call:
A serenade, a territorial challenge –
For it is only we
Who catch our breath at plaintive sadness for
Set of the sun, and coming on of night.

The Carrion Crow

A carrion crow sat on an oak
And watched where the line of battle broke.

A carrion crow sat on an ash –
He hears the spears' and shields' clash.

A carrion crow sat on a pine:
The long-bows are bent, the swift arrows whine.

A carrion crow sat on an elm:
The long sword batters the bright-plumed helm.

A carrion crow sat on a yew:
On Bosworth Field lies a crimson dew.

A carrion crow sat on a thorn,
Where the crown of England had rolled, forlorn.

The Rooks

The rooks in the rectory elm
Settle their disputes (or so it is said)
Convening a noisy parliament; always begin to build
On the same date in March – unless, indeed
It happens to fall on a Sunday.
They tolerate a few
Of those eccentric clowns, the jackdaws,
Among their company, but do not like
To be reminded of their cousins,
The carrion crows, out there on the heath
Living by scrounging and poaching:
'Oh no, of course, we never talk of those'.

The Jays

Two jays came down my street.
I heard them screeching, mate to his mate.
They kept well under cover, in hedge and shrubbery –
The bright, conspicuous, winged with azure,
Cinnamon-coloured birds.
I guess they were casing the joint.

From *Birds Reconvened* (1980)

The Greater Spotted Woodpecker

White-grey lichen on subfusc bark;
Chequered sunlight falls through twigs and leaves.
In this world of stipple and crosshatch the spotted woodpecker
(Who looks so conspicuous in the plate in your bird book)
Can move unseen. He spirals up a tree-bole,
Tapping and tapping for beetles and beetle-grubs;
Then beats out a tattoo – to call his mate
To come with a dipping flight through sun-splashed woodland rides –
Upon a hollow bough, his talking drum.

The Heron

An image remembered from boyhood – glimpsed
From a moving train: a pool,
Or else a brook which must have run perforce
Beside the tracks, and a heron standing,
Not in his grey stillness,
Watching the waters for his prey – but all in motion,
As he tries to get into his snaking gullet
A flapping, white-bellied, obstinate cuss of a fish.

The Curlew

Lord help all those lost up there tonight
From the treacherous bog, the precipice at their feet.
The mist lies low on the moors – and through it the calling,
The wild disconsolate calling. The cry of the whaup,
Men say it's unchancy.

The Wheatear

(for Shaun Traynor)

The green wheat is in the ear; in mediterranean vineyards
Vines have tiny flowers. On English down or wold
White Arse alights, a dweller in stony places:
'Excuse me, Brother Rabbit,
I need your spare accomodation.'

The Greenfinch

On a May morning,
In the greening time
I heard a greenfinch in a college garden
Set to his jargon in a leafy tree;
The long flat call-note, which will be repeated
Through all the hot and dusty days of summer,
Subsumed in a desultory twitter.
The lazy greenfinch, thick-set country cousin
Of the trim, suburban, caged canary –
Green, green, green he calls through the green leaves.

The Chaffinch

There's apple-blossom now, for Spring
Has made a definite entrance. With smoke-blue cap,
White epaulettes, and breast a rusty pink,
The chaffinch hurries through his rapid song:
So may some dowdier Mimi Pinson
Be quick quick quick quick quick quick quick to hear,
And Coelebs not be long a bachelor.

From *Birds Reconvened* (1980)

A Paraphrase

The raven and the crow,
They neither reap nor sow;
The magpie and the jay,
They don't make hay,
Nor do they cart their corn
Into the tithe barn:
Whom the Father's hand shall feed –
They find what they need.

The lenten daffodil,
Blowing beneath the hill,
And the bright briar-rose –
These do not want for clothes,
Nor do they ever throw
The shuttle to and fro:
No spindle and no loom
Forms the perfect bloom.

Great King Solomon,
With all his glory on,
Dressed up to the nines
Among his concubines,
Is not more fine to see
Than a wild anemone.

This Is Your Poem

This is your poem – an utterly useless present:
You can hang it up, or put it away in a drawer.
If the former, and the wind blows through it,
It will not give voice to any more beautiful chimes
Than now it does; and if the latter,
Mice may find it and make it into a nest –
But that is the only thing it will ever be good for.

You can make fine shreds of this paper, and steep them
In spirits of wine, but this will not mitigate
The fury of your toothache, nor is it recommended,
By the veterinary profession, for sick cattle,
Distempered fox-hounds, or egg-bound Dorkings.

Garlic and houseleek, collected
At the spring festival, will scare
The brood of Lilith from your threshold,
The hobgoblins and vampires. A holy icon
Can mediate the presence of the blessed saints.
This will do neither of these – it can only wish,
To you and your roof-tree, prosperity and kindness.
But if wishes were horses beggars would ride, and if
Poems were cadillacs poets would probably
Drive them to the public mischief.

Greensleeves

'Platonic England'
– Geoffrey Hill

for Leonard Clark

Knapweed, bindweed, scabious, burnet,
Sorrel, eyebright, elecampane,

Foxglove, lords and ladies, old man's beard –
I could continue this litany of flowers:

They are the sweetness blooms upon her face –
Merlin's glimmering isle,

Whose blood and bones and guts and sweat are coal,
Iron, methane, oil, lead:

White faces in slum alleys, rat faces,
Bodies bent with rickets, crouched in the mine.

On the train from Dover, disembarking from the packet
(Too much cheap French wine
Had made me prone to facile tears) as I gulped
On a plastic cup of stewed, black tea,
And stodgy, saccharine cake, she rose
In pink and white of Kentish apple-blossom.
'I am called Lady Greensleeves,' she said,
'I also can betray and break the heart.'

Timur

Timur the Lame (or Tamburlaine we call him)
Made in his youth a vow, they say,
That he would never wittingly cause pain
To any sentient being; once seriously distressed
For accidentally treading on an ant.

The last skull is the apex of the pyramid:
'My enemies,' he cried (it is the same
Pure-minded boy who weeps, inside the skin
Tanned by all the dry winds of the steppe)
'So contumacious and so obdurate –
They all deserve to die
For causing me to break my lovely vow!'

From *The Immolation of Aleph* (1985)

Nixon, the Cheshire Prophet

for Bernard Saint

Black hair, a low forehead,
Sallow skin, jutting teeth,
Broad shoulders, big hands – he did his work,
Enough of it, in the fields,
But had to be beaten often.
Generally silent – but when the boys
Tormented him, he would run after them,
Making loud noises, grab them by the throat,
Kick them and thump them, till he was called off.

But sometimes something would seize him – whether the moon's phase,
Or the wind in the right quarter caused it, nobody knew.
But he'd begin his prophecies, in a strange voice,
Chanting them, in rhymed verses.
Forseeing the future – but in a jumble
As in a dream out of time. He spoke
Of the bloody severed head of a king,
Of England possessed by iron men,
Another king, fleeing,
Casting his seal into the dark Thames,
Men grubbing in the mountain's bowels,
Great argosies tossed on the waves,
Full of gold and spices and chinaware,
The mills and the looms of Satan
Spread Northward over the hills of Lancashire;
And a fire in London, fire growing
From the small womb of a baker's oven,
And fire cast down from the sky by great black birds;
And generations of men afraid of fire –
A small seed of fire in the heart of the motes
Which are the atoms that, swirling, make up creation,
And fire in the marrow of our own bones;
And always of Famine, a greedy female skeleton
Striding over the land, grabbing the poor

And cramming them into her yellow chops.

After this he'd fall silent, and eat
Even more prodigiously than usual.
Munching the cheese and the crusts, chawing on bacon knuckles,
Slurping the broth and the beer. And then he'd sleep,
Curled up on the hearth-stone; like an animal.

The king, on a Northern progress, learnt of this.
He had him brought before him. The king looked at him.
Having heard of a prophet, he'd expected perhaps
Something more ethereal, like the Boy David,
Or maybe the youthful Baptist, in naked purity
With only a girdle of camel-skin
About his loins. Oh well –
It was no new thing for him to be disappointed.
Nixon looked up. He saw
A little man wrapped in furs. He had weak legs,
For two young courtiers supported him.
Both thought 'He slobbers, just like me.'

The king said 'Prophet, you shall come to London,
And sing in my ain palace – better there, than spreading wild ideas
Among the common sort. I need a prophet
To warn me against my enemies – those hellish Papists
That would hoist me sky-high with their bombards and petards;
And the black witches, that melt my image
Over a slow fire, or bury it,
A pin stuck through the heart, in the cauld slime of a pig-sty.
The queen and her ladies have run plain daft
After those new-fangled masques, cavorting
And tripping about like allegorical goddesses.
Though Master Jonson writes fine verses for them,
And Master Jones devises braw machines,
I think you'll gie us homelier entertainment.
So I'll bring you to London. You'll ride in my ain coach.'

But Nixon began to whimper and snivel, and cried
'No! No! No! don't send me to London!

I know I shall starve in that place. I cannot bear it,
The hunger, the hunger, the wolf's tooth in my guts,
The dryness, the dryness, the torture of thirst!'
'Hoots,' said the king, 'you'll no starve.
You shall dwell in my kitchens. My cook shall feed you
With kickshaws and sweeties from the queen's cupboard,
And my ain table. Marchpains and cheesecakes,
And sugar-plums and almonds, and roasted larks,
Venison cooked in pastry coffins.'

The king was as good as his word. Nixon was placed in the kitchens
But the cooks and the scullions soon regretted this:
He was always under their feet, and filching
The snipe and godwits off the spit,
The roasted apples sizzling on the hob,
Scoffing pies and pasties, and sticking
His fingers into frumenties and flummeries,
And then into the dripping-pan. So they put him in a hole –
It was a disused wine-cooling vault – and threw down scraps
From time to time, but not ungenerously.

The king will go hunt at Windsor, and the court go with him:
There was pulling down of hangings, and rolling up of carpets,
Plate and pewter stacked in chests,
And chairs and tables piled upon wagons, for the whole furniture
Must go off with the king.
In all this confusion, Nixon was forgotten:
He was snoring soundly, – the night before
The cook had thrown down to him three pounds of sausages
A ring of black pudding, and a whole plateful
Of stale mutton pasties. When he awoke
The kitchens were all empty. For days and days,
His cries reverberated through the vaults,
But fainter and fainter. At last there was silence –
Nixon, the veridical prophet, the touchstone, the truepenny,
The right-tongued prophet had starved to death –
Even as he foretold he would –
A small black rat in a black hole.

Souvenir of St Petersburg

Petersburg street – 1840s. At one end
The poet Batyushkov (he has gone mad)
Continually asks himself, out loud, the time;
And gives himself the identical answer:
'It is eternity.'
    At the other end, John Field,
Expatriate Irish, inventor of the nocturne (and it is said
His life was one long nocturne; he falls asleep
Even when giving piano lessons to
Young girls of the best families – stertorous
Drunken Dublin snores) has dropped his walking-cane.
Too lazy or too gross to stoop and pick it up, he stands and waits
Until some passer-by shall do it for him.
He waits and waits and waits.

From *The Immolation of Aleph* (1985)

The Pearl

In my 'forties days, of Soho and Fitzrovia,
The Bricklayers' Arms, affectionately known
To all its regulars as the Burglars' Rest,
Could serve a decent plate of fishcakes, or of shellfish.
I found a pearl in a mussel once
And showed it to the barman. He dropped it on the floor,
And being no bigger than a small pin's head
It was quite irrecoverable. This kind of thing
Tends to occur with all the pearls I get.

Epitaph for Julian Kollerstrom, Mathematician

Number he loved. He was too much alone,
Living in time. And now beneath this stone
His body lies. Trust that his soul may be
Where numbers pass into infinity.

To the memory of George Frederick Heath-Stubbs
1925–1983

These dry leaves upon your urn:
Do you hear me, brother? Do you hear me?
Do you hear me now?

Earthfruits I'm bringing, also
The immolated lamb.

Accepted, rejected? No reply –
Only the wind that stirs
Your ashes and the dust of Africa.

Moving to Winter

As I move, through autumn to winter, my life's house
Is Edmund Waller's cottage of the soul.
How chill, how pure, eternity shines through the chinks!
Yet, while my fire still burns, I'll proffer
Scraps of toasted cheese to the crickets –
My long-legged, whiskery poems, that chirp in the crannies,
Or hop about on the flagstones. And there'll be other visitants – an
    incognito
Angel or so, all my accustomed ghosts,
And, twirling his forked tail, pendunculate-eyed,
With sharp, nine-inch proboscis for a nose,
Not all malignant, the odd domestic bogle.

The Game of Love and Death

He cut. I shuffled. He began to deal.
'We'll play' said Death, 'our green baize table
Be the four-cornered world. And we have partners –
This one is mine – he's dummy.' 'And I know him –
He's your twin brother and his name is Sleep.'
'Some say they cannot tell us two apart;
And maybe that innocuous non-player
Is really Death, and I am nothing more
Than just a leering phantom in your dreams.'
'And who' said I 'is given me for partner?
This little yobbo, hauled in from his street game,
Improperly dressed in a pair of tattered pinions
And a quiver full of darts a tenuous G-string
Ties around his narrow downy loins?'

Death led the four of clubs, the Devil's four-poster;
But I had got the wish-card, nine of hearts.
And after that he played the Curse of Scotland.
I looked into my hand – it seemed a poor one:
The Kings were all the mean-faced Henry Tudor,
Grandson of devious Owen, and the Queens,
Desperately clutching at their fragile flowers,
Were all the sad Elizabeth of York.
The Jacks, in their flat caps of maintenance,
Were knaves, and unreliable. All of them feared
The King of Spades, his drawn and brandished sword.
And Death poured out a stream of spades – black Spanish blades,
Pointed inexorably against my breast.

As for my partner, what sort of game was his?
He spilled the heart's blood from our chalices.
He snapped our batons, and he squandered
All our small change of diamonds. Which was the Joker –
He or our opponent? I began to wonder.
Death laid another spade upon the table;

It was the nine, and followed by the ace.
Then all at once love played the ace of hearts,
And, 'Hearts are trumps!' he shouted – 'Always have been,
Ever since the founding of the world,
So you can grin on the other side of your face.'
'The other side of my face,' pale Death replied
'Perhaps is more like yours than men suppose.'
He has the last word always, that one. So
The game went on, and it is still proceeding.

Mary Magdalen, Martha and Lazarus in Provence

A ship sailed into shore –
Martha and Lazarus it bore
And Mary Magdalen.

Mary did penance in a cave,
Although she surely knew
That she had been forgiven,
And she would enter through the gates of heaven.

Martha converted the whole countryside.
She liked things tidy. She repressed
Tarasc, the horror,
Just like a cockroach in her Bethany kitchen.

But Mary in her damp and smelly cave,
Had learned to love the lively little roaches.

Their brother Lazarus was of the company,
And, having died already,
There was no message he could give
Excepting 'Death is nothing that you need to fear'.
To him it seemed so obvious
It almost became tedious,
And in the end he yawned, and went to sleep again.

The Mulberry Tree

'Good neighbour Michael Drayton, and you, Old Ben
Stepped up from London to our Warwickshire –
The air is balmy, so we'll drink tonight
Under my mulberry tree, and hear the chimes.'

But English April's treacherous. Good ale and wine,
However generous they boast themselves,
Lower the temperature. The lurking microbe
Is everywhere, and waiting for its chance.

Death's always bitter – and pneumonia,
Though not the worst, isn't a cosy end.
But this, at least, was after a good party –
Drinking with friends. And who wouldn't like to have been
A caterpillar among those mulberry leaves,
To catch some of the talk that drifted upwards,
And pass it on when one had turned a moth.

In Memory

A scruffy beer drinkers' club, a basement
In a side street off the Charing Cross Road –
No introductions, and no names exchanged.
And then my room, a cellar
Under the pavement, near Lancaster Gate.
He spoke of the outback, of Ned Kelly –
A wild colonial boy with do-it-yourself armour –
Reproached me for my self-indulgent guilt.
'Nailed upon your private cross,' he said.
And, after that – it was not satisfactory:
Neither of us exactly young – for him
Only the second time with another man, he told me.

But, later on, I recognised
(I was in America) his photo
Upon the cover of a magazine.
Unmistakeable the balding head,
The battered face, broad shouldered stocky body.
I wondered if we'd ever meet again,
And if we did by chance, would he remember,
Or take it as a threat? But that
Was three decades ago and some years more.
And now a voice upon the air-waves tells me
That he is gone. He's dead and celebrated,
And then they played an interview
Recorded some years back. But residence
In England had quite sandpapered away
All the Australian vowels. But I am grieving –
Grieving for a little twig of love
That never blossomed – could not, should not blossom,
Among the débris of my journey's sidewalk.

Apple Gripe

They woke as from a drug-induced slumber –
A dream of darkness, of fire that was the darkness,
And in their guts, the gripe of apples.

What had it promised, that sibilant voice,
That affable constrictor? Knowledge –
Knowledge that only gods rejoice in.
They fumbled in the catacombs of their brains
For intimations they'd not know before.
They found mortality – never again
Might they suppose joy would be termless;
They found their nakedness – and sex no longer
Would be uncomplex and without its hate.

Foreclosure of their lease had not
As yet been uttered. That would come, and then,
While Eden withered all about them,
With vagrant lagging steps, they'd take their way
Towards the gate which would be slammed behind them.

From *The Sound of Light* (1999)

Ten Kinds of Birds

For John Minihan

Ten different kinds of birds I have identified
By their calls and songs as we sit here
Under a darkening sky of June, drinking our wine.
It was the wheezing call of the greenfinch
Greeted me on my arrival;
The robin redbreast, that sang to us
All the long winter through, is hardly trying now –
I guess his brood is fledged and flown; from a fruit-tree near the house
The unpretentious song
Of the garden-warbler comes; the sparrow
Has only got one note, but he's working on it.
More eloquent the blackbird – there are two blackbirds
With adjoining territories – one answers
But not identically, the other's phrases –
Sweet and rich their songs. More shrill, more passionate,
A little way off, a thrush is singing also;
Farther still, perhaps at a copse's edge,
The foolish croodling of the wood-pigeon.

From the church tower, from time to time,
A party of jackdaws flies. They cruise round for a bit,
And then return. They talk to each other,
As is their custom: 'Let's keep together boys –
If there should happen to be a hawk around
She'd likely pick off a straggler.'
Now the not-quite English accents
Of the collared dove sound somewhere to the right.
It seems he woke a chaffinch up,
Who then repeated his rattling tattle,
Ending with a phrase that sounds like 'ginger beer'
And then fell silent. So it goes on and on
Till one by one sleep claims the birds
As it must soon claim us. As we go in

There is a last blackbird. With sombre plumes
And golden mouth, he flings his melody
Into the darkness –
So let it be with me, when the night comes.

Fitz and the Mouse

'Don't kill that mouse,' said Edward Fitzgerald
To the boy who read to him, being the original
Old man in a dry month etcetera.
'There's room in the universe for all three of us.'

Not Actaeon

Not Actaeon but Artemis
Pursued by tripe hounds which her own flesh bred.

31st August 1997

Mary Kingsley and the Crocodile

While Mary Kingsley was crossing a lake
In her canoe, a crocodile
Attempted to climb into it. She hit him
With her paddle, and he retired.
Only twelve foot long, it was a young crocodile,
She explained afterwards, that hadn't yet learned manners.

And, navigating now the singing lake,
I can perceive much similar beasticles,
And they all want to get into the boat.

A Dream Transcribed

Memory of Philip Larkin

Blind as a bed-post I've been, for thirty years or more –
Yet still I dream in images, though now
They're fainter and less easy to remember
Than once they were. And thus, the other night,
I seemed to be travelling northward in a train
To one of those dull Midland towns, where once
He lived and worked. I got out at a station
Where he met me, in a kindly way.
We went to some place where there was a meal –
Either a restaurant, or his apartment.
Waking, I recalled how he had died –
And that was years ago – and how
We'd once been friends – in Oxford days,
And, when we'd both gone down, exchanged letters
Comparing notes on trying to find a job, which he likened
To one of those bicycle races, in which
The first to fall off is a winner. And then
I knew this dream of mine referred to
That world beyond death which, if such things are,
I must be drawing closer to. And to which, he,
Lying sleepless through a long tedious night,
So passionately refused his credence.

Ancient Wisdom

There was a Chinese sage, so I'm informed,
Deplored the invention of the wheelbarrow –
It led to immorality, he said,
It made it easier for younger folk
From different villages to meet, trundling
Their loads of night-soil to far-off locations.

In the Porcelain Factory

Once I was shown around a porcelain factory,
One of our best English producers of fine china
But what I remember best is a small man –
Hunchbacked he seemed or deformed in some way,
His only task to paint images of birds on cups or saucers.
This he did constantly and continually,
Not pausing to notice those of us who gazed at him.
I do not know if there was anyone to love him or to care for him.
His whole life this constant repetition
Of small images of love and song and freedom.
He must be gone now and who will remember him?

Three Translations from Giacomo Leopardi

The Evening After the Holy Day

The night is soft and clear and no wind blows;
The quiet moon stands over roofs and orchards
Revealing from afar each peaceful hill.
Beloved, now every alleyway is silent;
At intervals along the balconies
The night-long lantern gleams; you are asleep,
And gently slumber now gathers about
Your quiet chamber, and no single care
Gnaws at your heart; you do not know at all,
Nor think that you have opened in my breast
A very grievous wound. You are asleep:
And I have come abroad now to salute
The sky whose aspect seems to be so gentle,
And ancient Nature powerful over all,
Who has fashioned me for trouble. 'I deny
All hope to you,' she has said, 'yea, even hope;
Your eyes shall not be bright for any cause,
Except with weeping.' This was a festal day:
And you are resting after its delights;
And maybe in your dreams you still remember
How many eyes took pleasure in your beauty,
How many, too, pleased you: I find no place –
Not that I hoped it now – among your thoughts.
Meantime I ask how many years of life
Remain to me, and therefore here I cast
Myself upon the ground, and cry, and rage.
Oh terrible days, even of our green youth!
Alas, I hear not far along the road

The lonely singing of a workman, coming
Back to his poor home so late at night,
After the sports; and fiercely my heart aches
Thinking how all this world passes away
And leaves no trace. For look, the festival
Is over now, an ordinary day
Succeeds tomorrow; all things our race has known
Time likewise bears away. Where now is the voice
Of the ancient peoples, the clamour of our ancestors
Who were renowned, and that great Empire of Rome,
The arms, and the clash they made by lands and sea?
All is silence and peace; the world is still;
There are no tidings now remain of them. Jo
Once in my boyhood, when so eagerly
We would look forward to the holiday,
Finding it over, I lay upon my bed,
Wakeful and very unhappy; late at night
A singing heard along the alleyways,
Little by little dying into the distance,
Even as this does now, gripped at my heart.

(1819)

To the Moon

O gracious Moon, I call to mind again
It was a year ago I climbed this hill
To gaze upon you in my agony;
And you were hanging then above that wood,
Filling it all with light, as you do now.
But dim and tremulous your face appeared,
Seen through the tears that rose beneath my eyelids,
My life being full of travail; as it is still –
It does not change, O my sweet Moon. And yet
Remembrance helps, and reckoning up
The cycles of my sorrow. How sweet the thought
That brings to mind things past, when we are young –
When long's the road for hope, for memory brief –
Though they were sad, and though our pain endures.

(1819)

The Younger Brutus

What time uprooted in the Thracian dust
Lay, an immense ruin
Italy's virtue, from whence the Fates prepared
For green Hesperia's vales and Tiber's banks
Tramp of barbarian horse, and from stark forests,
Oppressed by the frozen Bear,
To the destruction of Rome's famous walls,
Called forth the Gothic swords;
Worn out and dripping with his kindred's blood
Brutus, in blackest night seated alone,
Resolute now on his own death, accused
Avernus and the inexorable Powers, and thus with savage accents,
Vainly made tremulous the drowsy air.

'Stupid Virtue, the hollow clouds, the fields
Haunted by unquiet ghosts –
These are your schools, and at your back comes round
Bitter remorse. To you, marmoreal Powers,
(If Powers there be in hold of Phlegethon
Or here beneath the clouds), a laughing-stock
And scorn is our sad race
From whom you beg temples and with fraudulent laws,
Insult mortality.
Is Heaven's hatred then so much provoked
By earthly piety? Do you, Jove, sit
Impiety's protector? And when exults
The cloudburst through the air, and when
Hurtles the rapid thunder,
Whelm on the good and just your sacred fires?

Unconquerable Fate and iron
Necessity bear down
Upon the sickly slaves of Death; no intermission
Availing for his outrage, the common man
Consoles himself that ills are necessary.

Is the irreparable less harsh? Is grief unfelt
By him who's stripped of hope?
War to the death, eternal, the brave soldier
Wages with you, base Fate,
Not schooled to yield; and with the tyrannous grip
Of your right hand, victorious on him laid,
Shrugs it off unsubdued, with a last gesture
When in his own proud flank
The bitter steel makes entry,
And grimly smiles toward the blackening shades.

Displeasing to the gods is he, who violent, storms
The underworld: such valour
Is not for their feeble, eternal breasts.
The Heavens perhaps devised our sufferings,
Our bitter lot and our tormented passions,
As a mere spectacle to please their sight.
Calamities nor crimes,
But free, unsullied ages in the woods,
Nature ordained for us,
Our queen and goddess once. Now when on earth
Impious custom wrecks her hallowed reign,
Our meagre life kept back by other laws,
When one of manly soul
Rejects the ill-omened days,
Will Nature blame his dart as not her own?

They know no guilt, nor their own suffering,
The fortunate wild herds;
Calmly, their latter age leads on apace
Without foreknoweledge. But if distress should urge them
To dash their heads on the rough trunks, or to consign
From mountain rocks their bodies headlong down
Into the wind, no arcane law
Nor dark conceit stands to contend against
Their wretched longings. You, among so many
Stocks Heaven vivifies, for you alone,
Son of Prometheus, life is a torment;

And Jove to you alone
Forbids, O wretched men,
If tardy Fate delays, the shores of death.

And you, pale moon, rising out of the sea
Our blood incarnadines,
Survey the unquiet night, and these sad plains,
Ill-fated for the might of Italy.
The victor tramples on his kinsmen's hearts;
The hills are loud, from topmost summits ruins
Rome's antique glory down;
And do you watch so calmly, you who saw
The Latin nation's birth, the joyful years
And all its memorable laurels won?
And you, silent above the Alps shall shed
Your still unaltering beams, when mid the wrongs
Of Italy's servile name
That solitary seat
Is deafened by the tramp of barbarous feet.

Among the naked rocks, on the green bough,
The beast and wild bird
In customary oblivion of sleep
Know not the deep ruin nor the changed
State of the world; and when the labouring peasant's
Rooftop is touched by crimson of the dawn,
With morning canticles
The one will wake the valleys, and the other
From the high cliffs
Startle the weaker droves of lesser animals.
Condition vain, vain race of man, we are
The abject part of things! Neither the bloodstained soil
Nor the rebellowing caves
Has our disaster troubled,
Nor does the human anguish dim the stars.

Neither to you, Olympus, nor the deaf
Lords of Cocytus, nor to unworthy Earth,

Nor, dying, to the night, do I appeal;
Nor you, the last beam gleaming through black death,
Conscious posterity. Shall the vile crowd's
Sobs placate my arrogant tomb, their words
And offerings deck it out? From bad to worse
The times rush on; not well it is we assign
To our corrupt descendants
The honour of outstanding minds, their woes'
Ultimate vindication. Let the dark bird,
Whose pinions are about me, greedily tear;
Let the beast prey, and the rain cloud
Draw up the unnoted spoils,
The wind receive my name and memory.'

(December, 1821)